COLLIN

G000107878

WALK LOCH L
AND THE TROSSACHS

by Gilbert Summers

HarperCollins*Publishers*

Published by Collins
An imprint of HarperCollins*Publishers*
77-85 Fulham Palace Road
London W6 8JB

Copyright © HarperCollins*Publishers* Ltd 1988
Text © Gilbert Summers 1998
Maps © Bartholomew Ltd 1988

First published by Bartholomew 1986
Revised 1988, 1990
Reprinted 1992
Reprinted with amendments 1994, 1996
First published by Collins 1998
Reprinted 1999

The landscape is changing all the time. While every care has
been taken in the preparation of this guide, the Publisher accepts
no responsibility whatsoever for any loss, damage, injury or
inconvenience sustained or caused as a result of using this guide.

Printed in Hong Kong

ISBN 0 00 448699 4

86/4/81.5

CONTENTS

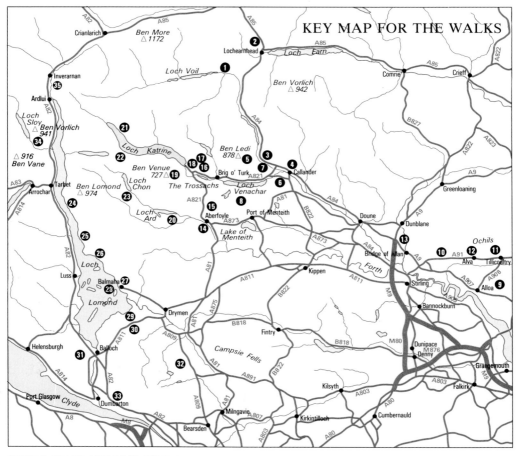

KEY MAP FOR THE WALKS

KEY TO SCALE AND MAP SYMBOLS

SCALE 1 : 63360

SCALE 1 : 25000

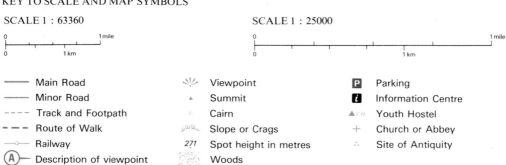

——	Main Road	☀ Viewpoint	▣ P Parking
——	Minor Road	▲ Summit	▣ i Information Centre
- - - -	Track and Footpath	ᴖ Cairn	▲ᵞᴴ Youth Hostel
- - -	Route of Walk	⏦ Slope or Crags	+ Church or Abbey
⊶⊶	Railway	*271* Spot height in metres	∴ Site of Antiquity
Ⓐ—	Description of viewpoint	Woods	

4

1 WHY LOCH LOMOND AND THE TROSSACHS...?

The appeal of the area covered by this book has been known for generations. In the most general sense, what William Wordsworth did for Lakeland, Sir Walter Scott also achieved with the Trossachs. The two areas have several similarities, not the least of which has been a more or less reverent pilgrimage to sites identified with both poets by visitors who have probably never willingly read Wordsworth or Scott in their lives. The second and obvious similarity is the nearness of both the English Lakes and the Scottish Trossachs to major centres of population. It was perfectly reasonable for the Trossachs and Loch Lomond to be 'discovered' early in scenic sense - not only are they outstanding areas of natural beauty, but they represent the flavour of the Highlands within a short journey of the densely populated lowlands.

But in the final account, a hard grandeur, a troubled history and a (sometimes slightly eerie) sense of emptiness ensures that Loch Lomond and the Trossachs are uniquely Scottish. This book is for ordinary walkers who want a chance to stretch their legs in the fresh air, perhaps a place to park that does not make the driver feel uneasy, and a day out without too many worries about the uncomfortable questions of access, route-finding - or getting back in time for tea.

Reaching the area is easy. Central Scotland's motorway network places Stirling well under an hour from both Glasgow and Edinburgh. Further to the east, the Kincardine Bridge gives fast access to the Ochils walks, while westwards, Aberfoyle by the A81 or Loch Lomond from the A82 are both trouble-free routes. Edinburgh and Glasgow are also departure points for bus connections or trains to Stirling or Arrochar.

2 WALKING IN THE LOCH LOMOND AND TROSSACHS AREA - AND FURTHER EAST

This is an area of contrast. The choice of walks reflects this. Not all of them are Highland. Routes on and near the Ochils east of Stirling have been included, not only as a foretaste of more heathery hills further west, but as interesting viewpoints in themselves. Even the more industrial lowlands have not been entirely neglected. Gartmorn Dam, near Alloa, provides a fine level walk where early industrial development has been replaced by a stretch of water much appreciated by high numbers of birds, while Overtoun near Dumbarton shows how easy it is to escape into the moors.

The Callander area to the north-east provides another focal point. Many visitors will be surprised to find how easy it is to escape the busy tourist streets. In this area is the highest of the walks, to the summit of Ben Ledi. The northern borders of the area covered are reached on a walk taking advantage of a disused railway in Glen Ogle.

In the centre of the area covered, in addition to forestry roads and tracks, advantage has been taken of the surfaced road round Loch Katrine. The Trossachs are explored from many angles, wherever access permits.

Loch Lomond, with its rugged and steeper terrain in the north and tendency to sprout 'private' notices in the south, has been covered partly by dipping into the West Highland Way, Scotland's first long-distance footpath. In this rugged area in particular, the walks have been chosen with care, bearing in mind the relatively inexperienced walker. Equally, they have been chosen to make the most of Loch Lomond's famed beauty -islands dot its water, Ben Lomond looms impressively on its eastern shore, and secret places still survive surprisingly close to the rush of traffic along the A82.

The selection is intended to be representative, rather than exhaustive - there are many more routes for walkers to discover for themselves. Though varying in length, the suggested routes have one feature in common - they should all be suitable for the reasonably fit walking party, wearing stout shoes or boots with well-cleated soles.

3 WHAT TO WEAR IN THE SCOTTISH COUNTRYSIDE - VARIED WEATHER PATTERNS

This section is not intended as a guide to what the sartorially-conscious walker will wear this season. (Most walkers are fairly idiosyncratic anyway and never stray far without their beloved woolly hat and sweater.) Winter walkers would be well advised to take an anorak or thick jacket, woolly hat, scarf, gloves and waterproof over-trousers. Inner clothing should comprise several thin layers, rather than one thick jumper, and warm trousers, NOT jeans. As regards footwear, proper walking boots are preferable and, for some walks, essential, particularly where the individual texts mention wet or slippery paths. Even if boots are not worn, shoes *must* give good ankle support and have a well-cleated sole to provide grip. Country lanes and idyllic meadows are in short supply - replaced by terrain on a grander scale.

Summer walkers still need strong footwear, plus a light cagoule-type jacket, a spare sweater - and, summer, or not, the waterproof trousers or lightweight rain-suit might still be useful. Remember the vagaries of Scottish weather. Stunning colours, tumbling streams, lovely lochs mean, after all, water, in the form of rainfall that increases the further west you go,

complicated by further increases the higher you climb. Mid-March to mid-June is, as the most daring of generalisations, often the driest period, though, personally speaking, September and October have much to recommend them. July and August are warmer, but statistically wetter. Remember, too, the rule of thumb that for each 1000ft (305m) climbed, there will be a drop of around 4 degrees F., with windspeeds likewise increasing. The best advice on clothing, therefore, is to be flexible. The average July temperature is around 58-59 degrees F. (14.44-15 degrees C.). Where a walk would be less than rewarding in bad weather, that is, where the loss of a view outweighs the interest level of the immediate surroundings, then this is mentioned in the individual texts. Ben Cleuch in the Ochils, Ben An in the Trossachs are a couple of examples.

A small word about a small problem - the infamous Highland Midge. Some visitors may have mused that there must have been a conspiracy of silence over this less-than-endearing feature of life in the Highlands. Certainly, few glossy tourism brochures give it any space, but it is fair to point out that in still conditions, on mild days near bodies of water in particular, the uniformly sadistic members of the Ceratopogonidae family may make their presence felt. Long-sleeved shirts are therefore preferable, and you are advised to carry a repellent, which usually needs frequent re-application. Different people react in differing degrees to their bites, but the attentions of any of the twenty-nine different blood-sucking species can be a little annoying.

4 SAFETY FIRST IN THE SCOTTISH COUNTRYSIDE

It is always wise to have additional maps, covering a wider area than the intended walk and hence useful for identifying distant features. The 1:50 000 OS series is recommended, as is the OS Tourist Map of Loch Lomond and the Trossachs, while enthusiasts will appreciate the extra detail of the 1:25 000 series. A compass is also useful - essential if you deviate from these recommended routes. A plastic bag for maps is a good idea, or even better, a proper plastic map-holder with a cord strap as used by orienteering enthusiasts.

Learn the basics of map-reading. At least be able to orientate yourself by holding the compass on top of the map, folded to the relevant portion, and turning map, compass and yourself until the compass needle points to magnetic north. You should then be able to identify features in the landscape. If you do not have a compass then from a known point, line up the map with a more distant feature, such as a hill-top.

In assessing how long each walk should take, it is difficult to generalise - your decision-making must be based on the slowest member of the party. Pay most attention to the vertical rise given for some of the walks and allow extra time. Do not assume that the shortest distance will take the shortest time. For example, compare Ben An (Walk 17) with Falls of Leny (Walk 7). The lengths look the same but the first requires twice as much time, fitness and care as the second. Remember that all of the walks described are intended to be pleasurable outings - not too taxing and designed to allow for picnics, photography, botany, birdwatching and gazing at the views! If in doubt, choose a there-and-back again route and clearly note your starting time.

Many walkers, particularly if going high in winter, leave notes on the car dashboard with their routes and estimated return times. Although the walks in this book are generally modest in scale, do not feel embarrassed about adopting this practice. Likewise, let someone know at 'base' where you intend to go. Read each walk before you start off and pay close attention to warnings, particularly if boisterous children are in the party. Without dwelling overmuch on the gloomy aspects of the Scottish landscape, remember that smooth wet grass, twisted heather roots, old leaves, are all hazards even before you encounter the more obvious crags, rocky places, fast-flowing streams, slippery banks of lochs and other obstacles which contribute to the unique beauty of the Highlands.

A small first aid kit is invaluable for treating the occasional small cuts and bruises, and a whistle is useful for attracting attention should a more serious accident occur. If someone in the party does meet with an accident, ensure that when you reach a telephone, you give as precise details as possible of the location to the police and emergency services. But, to repeat, constant watchfulness is the best way to avoid this possibility, particularly as the walk nears its end and tired legs are less able to avoid pitfalls.

5 HOW THE WALKS ARE GRADED

Given that all the area can be described as rugged, to a greater or lesser extent, this leads on to the question of grading the walks. To take the Ben Ledi example, at under 3000 ft, it might be considered an easy jaunt for a party of fit hillwalkers, accustomed to relentless gradients. For the ordinary family on holiday it would present more of a challenge - which is why it is labelled 'Strenuous' in this book. At the other extreme, even if a walk is graded 'Easy', remember that you are in Scotland, and that it is still advisable to be properly equipped.

The area, rather obviously, has lots of steep gradients - for those who seek them. However, to make for more relaxed walking, advantage has often been taken of the astonishing mileage of forestry roads in the area. Some of these have been waymarked by the Forestry Commission and this book takes the liberty of joining in and opting out of these markers to suit the purpose of the walk. Remember on the Forestry Commission's ground that their own activities may, from time to time, mean a particular route is temporarily out of bounds. Do not worry - there is a wide choice. Instead ponder upon the problems that might be encountered if there was not normally a fairly liberal attitude taken in Scotland to the crossing of land in private ownership.

6 THE LAW OF TRESPASS IN SCOTLAND

Read all the available literature on walking in Scotland and you can be forgiven for still feeling a little hazy on the question of the rights of the individual walker. At one extreme there appear in print little guides which urge the determined walker to carry a thick polythene bag to help cross barbed-wire. One even suggests that in certain areas, the walker with a picnic would be well advised to choose a dense thicket in which to consume it! Other texts dismiss the whole business and blithely state that there is no law of trespass north of the border. This is incorrect. The law of trespass in Scotland concerns itself with possible damage while the trespasser is on private land. In practical terms, this means the onus is on the landowner to prove damage -but he or she is entitled to request you to leave his or her land by the shortest practical route.

Some of these walks take advantage of rights of way, which in Scotland are defined as routes between places of 'public resort' in use for a period of at least twenty years. However, the lack of certainty over the whole business has partly come about through the tolerant attitude shown by many landowners on the question of walkers on their land. Should you, while using this book, go wrong and stray from the recommended routes, you then bear full responsibility for ensuring that this fairly satisfactory relationship between most landowners and walkers in Scotland is maintained. Check locally for seasonal or temporary restrictions such as lambing or stalking. Your local Tourist Information Centre or Countryside Ranger Service will be able to assist.

7 THE COUNTRY CODE

Most walkers are responsible people, showing the appropriate degree of common sense with regard to countryside activities. Nevertheless, here is a reminder: the Country Code - as laid down by the Countryside Commission:

1 Enjoy the countryside and respect its life and work
2 Guard against all risk of fire
3 Fasten all gates
4 Keep your dogs under close control
5 Keep to public paths across farmland
6 Use gates and stiles to cross fences, hedges and walls
7 Leave livestock, crops and machinery alone
8 Take your litter home
9 Help to keep all water clean
10 Protect wildlife, plants and trees
11 Take special care on country roads
12 Make no unnecessary noise

Study the code closely and you will find it is a perfectly reasonable list of suggestions, imposing nothing whatsoever on the recreational countryside user. One or two aspects of it are particularly important for the area covered by this book. Keeping dogs under proper control is of great importance as many of the walks are in sheep country. Remember that under the *Civic Government (Scotland) Act* 1982 a farmer may shoot a dog which is about to attack livestock if there is no other means of restraining it at that moment. The law is on the farmer's side as he may then prosecute and claim damages from you as its erring owner for any injury or loss. (Roe deer, when very young, are also vulnerable to injury from roaming dogs.) You can see why it is simpler to keep your impetuous pet on a lead - and pay close attention to any warning notices in the lambing season.

Young birds, when just out of the nest, can draw attention to themselves by weak flight and unnatural tameness. Leave well alone - their parents will be along shortly with their next meal. And under the general heading of respect for wildlife and the countryside, do not disturb the nesting site of any wild bird. Similarly, picking wild flowers is frowned upon most severely - it is downright selfish anyway - and you might just meet a militant botanist.

Worth emphasising, too, is that surprisingly early in the year, forests can become a fire hazard and common sense must be exercised. Remember that your host for many of these walks is the Forestry Commission. Read their notices carefully.

Many of these walks are also accessible by permission of Strathclyde Water Board, a major landowner all round Loch Katrine. The city of Glasgow depends on Loch Katrine and its neighbours for its water supply. Some of the walks trace the course of the Victorian engineering feats that made this resource available to Scotland's major conurbation. For the walker it means that the landscape is well preserved and relatively undisturbed by developments, but this unspoilt aspect for the sake of pure water means that boating, bathing and other potentially polluting activities are restricted in the environs of the lochs. Make sure you remember this. Visit the Loch Katrine exhibition at the Trossachs car park, open during the summer months, for the full story.

8 GEOLOGY AND LANDSCAPE

The Highland Boundary Fault lies across the area covered in this book. It will be noticeable on many of the walks that the views give Highland and lowland contrasts. The fault line that separates the Highlands from the Scottish Midland Valley runs through Loch Lomond, Balmaha, the Menteith Hills, Loch Venachar and on, north-eastwards. Below it, the immediate lowlands are mainly sandstone on which very recent glacial action has dumped other rocks and gravels, though the Ochils are built of ancient lavas, also present less significantly in the Menteith Hills. Northwards, complicated bands of conglomerate, slates, and schistose grits are not easily comprehended by the amateur eye. As a simplification, it is enough to remember that the northern rock types are harder and more resistant to weathering than the sandstones immediately to the south. These northern Dalradian rocks (named after Dalradia, the first Scottish kingdom) are variable in appearance, some still showing their gritty origins on the floors of ancient seas, while others through heat and pressure have 'metamorphosed'. Probably the commonest are the schists, grey in appearance, sometimes streaked with parallel bands of other minerals.

The present-day landscape owes much to the differing degrees of hardness of these rocks, with the most resistant schistose grits forming the conspicuous bulk of Ben Lomond and Ben Ledi. After these ancient rock movements, much more recent Ice Ages (the last as recent as 10,000 years ago) stripped and plucked at the rough shapes, deepening and scouring valleys, dumping and damming to create major lochs such as Loch Lomond. Now, modern man has wrought other basic landscape changes. Electric power and water supply needs have resulted in the tampering with Lochs Sloy, Venachar, Katrine, Arklet, Drunkie and a few other waters in the vicinity.

9 HISTORY

Once, most of the area north of the Highland Boundary Fault was truly 'Highland' in the sense that its Celtic population lived by an economy adapted to a mountainous terrain. The clan system meant that families in any one community owed allegiance to the local chief. Some of the families would hold land as 'tacksmen' or relatives of the chief, others would pay rent in turn to these tacksmen. This system had evolved by about the mid 13th century. There was both a physical mountain barrier and a language separating these tribal units from the lowlands to the south.

Just over the barrier, the feudal barons were powerful. For example, Doune Castle, near Callander, was the centre of a large block of territory, held in the name of the Dukes of Albany. In those very distant times, the Earls of Lennox held sway over the south end of Loch Lomond from an earlier Balloch Castle. The Menteith Grahams were powerful in the area between. There is no space here to pursue the complexities of the area's history, but it must be said that the lowland landowners were not always successful in keeping the Highland clansmen from raiding southwards. Besides, for many of them, there were political careers to pursue elsewhere. News from their own tenants that yet another score of cattle had vanished into the mountains was extremely inconvenient. Things became so bad along the Highland/lowland border that, on occasion, the Scottish kings were even asked to intervene. From

Edinburgh's Holyrood House in 1585 an edict was issued, summoning the local landowners to Stirling: 'The King and his council, being informed that his good and peaceable subjects inhabiting the countries of Lennox, Menteith, Stirlingshire and Strathearn are heavily oppressed by reif, stouth and sorning and other crimes daily and nightly'. The three unfamiliar words mean plundering, theft and squatting - the last mentioned also involved using weapons to fend off any attempt to collect rent.

At one time 'sorning' was a particular problem in Balquhidder Glen, though by the 17th century the glen was nominally controlled by the Murray family with headquarters in far away Blair Castle. Unquestionably, north of the Highland line, life was hard - little wonder that black cattle were lifted with regularity from the lowland fields. They provided a kind of 'welfare state' on the hoof - a handy currency to see a family through a bad winter. One clansman who appreciated this from an early age was a certain Rob Roy Macgregor.

10 ROB ROY MACGREGOR

The Kirkton Glen walk (Walk 1) starts from Rob Roy's graveside, while the Loch Katrineside excursion (Walk 21) is to the scene of his childhood. He was born in Glen Gyle of the Clan Gregor, who at the time were being tolerated by a monarchy which had actually outlawed the entire clan earlier in the century, for the kind of reasons mentioned in section 9. His career cannot be separated from the time in which he lived. The reign of the Stuart monarchy was ending. Born in 1671, as a teenager, Rob would hear of the succession of the House of Hanover, yet he remained a Jacobite (a supporter of the Stuart claimants) all his life, no doubt acquiring these sympathies from an early age through his own father who served in the army of the Stuart King Charles II.

He is remembered today, not just through the romantic portrait painted by Sir Walter Scott in his novel Rob Roy, but partly because in those lawless times, he, in effect, challenged the government, which in spite of all the resources of the 'British' army, was unable to bring him in. Sir Walter certainly saw him as the symbol of a Highland way of life, proud and independent, that was to vanish utterly with the advance of lowland 'civilisation' and the final dismantling of the clan system after Culloden in 1746.

The 'real' Rob Roy rose to notoriety through his

dealings in the cattle trade, as a semi-legitimate drover, dealer and opportunist with one eye on the lowland herds. Superb swordsmanship, survival skills and hill craft enabled him to defend property on the hoof, both his own and his 'clients'. This was noticed by the very powerful Duke of Montrose, who owned substantial grounds around Loch Lomond (and was a Hanoverian, too). A deal was struck. Rob was to use the Duke's money to buy and fatten cattle, with profits shared. However, the money disappeared while in the hands of one of Rob's own trusted drovers. Rather than give Rob time to repay the funds and with the most questionable of motives (Rob owned some lands on the east bank of Loch Lomond - now crossed by the West Highland Way, the Duke promptly declared him an outlaw and seized his house and lands. Thus, in 1712, a desperate phase of the Macgregor's life began.

He was, after all, 'hot property' - a man of skill and craft in an unstable political climate. He was within the sphere of operations of not only Montrose, but also another baron of high office - the Duke of Argyll, who was to command the government forces against the rebel Jacobites at Sheriffmuir three years later. (You are near the battle site on the Dumyat walk.) Rob played a large part in this rebellion. Montrose wanted him to implicate Argyll in a Jacobite plot, with the return of Rob's lands if he bore false witness against Argyll, Montrose's political opponent.

He refused and instead redoubled his raiding on Montrose lands. He was captured on more than one occasion, but always managed to escape. Another major landowner, the Duke of Atholl, even managed to capture him through treachery, but Rob escaped again and made his way to Balquhidder. A network of sympathisers and intelligence gatherers, plus supreme survival skills, meant that Rob, even after playing a part in the rebellion at Glenshiel in 1719, could gradually re-emerge to pursue the life of a cattle dealer, with a little semi-legitimate protectionism, in Balquhidder. There was eventually a reconciliation between all parties and Rob was to die peacefully in 1734. In his years of hardship as a fugitive, he paid the price for his refusal to become a part of lowland power squabbles, while remaining true to the Jacobite cause and evading all attempts to be brought to lowland justice.

Consider this as you stand on the slopes of Ben Ledi on Walk 5. Stirling Castle is on the near horizon, from where the nervous government garrisons would have been despatched following yet another rumour that the freebooter had been seen locally. Just above Loch Lubnaig, to the north, is Balquhidder, where Rob had sympathisers in plenty. North and south were two worlds, separated by language, customs and geography and only forcibly united when communications improved - the military road can still be traced above the Pass of Leny.

11 THE LITERARY LANDSCAPE AND TOURISM

To Sir Walter, talking on his journeys to old men who claimed as very young children actually to have seen the revered Macgregor, here was the stuff of romance. Daniel Defoe thought so too, even earlier. (He would have heard such tales while living in Edinburgh, covertly helping with a spy ring which sent back information to Queen Anne, on the unrest in Scotland after the country lost its independence in 1707.) His *Adventures of a Highland Rogue* had assured Rob of fame in his own lifetime. But Scott could see, as he travelled in the area, that here was a land of vanished people, of a way of life that had no place as society was swept into the Industrial Revolution. His Rob Roy, symbolic of courage and honour, confronts a Baillie Nichol Jarvie representing lowland commerce and industry.

Scott was writing at a time of transition for the area. Though complex, the changes mainly came about through the impact of agricultural improvements in the lowlands, on a land already suffering from the aftermath of the post-Culloden political and social upheaval in the last half of the 18th century. Of the northern landowners, some with Jacobite loyalties had their lands forfeited after Culloden, while the rest were keen on introducing changes to the glens. The day of the black-face and cheviot sheep had arrived. Pasture that had grown oats and fed cattle for mainly local consumption was now nibbled down by ubiquitous sheep. Timber was cut to improve the sheep-walks. The creation of larger farms needing less labour meant that the glens soon emptied and emigration got under way, either to cities or overseas - after all, a laird or chieftain now had no need to be able to call on numbers of armed kinsmen to defend his holdings.

Thus, when the Wordsworths visited the Trossachs on their Highland Tour in 1803, they already found an empty land. They clearly contributed to the cult of landscape and were impressed in particular with the startling contrast between Loch Achray with its meadows and the wildness that lay through the narrow defile below Ben An, as they entered the heart of the Trossachs. (Compare the peaceful setting of Loch Ard with the wildness seen westward from the top of Ben An on Walk 17.) James Hogg journeyed here, too, and there were other travel narratives describing the wonders of this region on the edge of the mountains, even before the publication of Scott's *The Lady of the Lake* in 1810. It proved so successful that tourists flocked to see the sights and pick out the landscape features. Tourism was well under way.

Queen Victoria's love for the Highlands helped promote the fashion of visiting Scotland. In various parts of the country, the sporting possibilities of the moors were developed. Landowners could make money by leasing the land to sporting tenants, with any humbler tenants still remaining employed as ghillies. But as 20th-century wars and economic slumps also took their toll, these vast uplands were to prove simply not profitable.

12 FORESTRY...AND MORE TOURISM

Forestry was the solution chosen to improve the fortunes of an upland area in decline. Now, along with a highly developed tourism industry, sweeping landscape changes have again taken place. There are historical precedents - the earlier Dukes of Montrose planted oak woods extensively in the Aberfoyle area. The bark was used in the tanning industry, itself obviously dependent on cattle. Now the state-owned Queen Elizabeth Forest Park, established in 1953, clothes the central area in the glaucous green of conifers. The acquisition of land of high landscape, but poor economic, value by the Forestry Commission started around the Trossachs and Loch Lomond areas in the 1920s.

The planting methods involve the ploughing of deep furrows and the placing of each young tree in the resultant upturned mound. You will see hill slopes where this activity has been quite recent and others where felling is under way, at time of writing, for

example, above Loch Lubnaig. The dominant species are sitka and Norway spruce, with some Scots and lodgepole pines on the drier areas. The walker will also find other firs and some oak and beech plantings, as well as semi-natural oak woods and birch scrub, the latter an indicator of the kind of landscape which would initially regenerate were it not for the sheep and deer.

It is no easy matter, coaxing economic returns on rocky slopes often deficient in phosphate and essential nutrients. Local populations of red and roe deer do not assist in this task, which is why deer-proof fences are often to be encountered, but at most places in the routes suggested in this book you will find deer-proof stiles, too. The walker, deep in the wind-rocked silence of tall pines, would be incorrect to assume that the trees around have been ignored since seedling stage. Far from it - cross drains go into the ploughed lands, then thinning takes place around twenty years later, and continues every five years until clear-felling is carried out after about fifty years of growth. Fertilizing or spraying may also be necessary - as well as the building of access roads for plantation maintenance and extraction. Yet in spite of all that, the forests are peaceful places - and at least half of the walks detailed in this book pass through Forestry Commission property at some point.

Modern leisure needs overlap fairly well with forestry activities. The coach parties gazing from the Duke's Road above Aberfoyle are quite satisfied with the moorlands well-spiked by spruce at various stages of maturity. Car parks, picnic sites and forest trails are much in evidence from Loch Lomond to Callander Crags. Under countryside legislation the Forestry Commission is, in fact, bound to 'have regard to the desirability of conserving the natural beauty and amenity of the countryside'. This is why there are few problems of access on its land, unless it conflicts with management activities, such as spraying or felling. Right across the area, there is a constant reminder of the statistic that eighty per cent of new planting in Britain is in Scotland - and the Queen Elizabeth Forest Park plays its part.

Walk 1
KIRKTON GLEN
5 miles (8km) + 1540ft (470m) Moderate

Speedy travellers on the main road between Strathyre and Lochearnhead sometimes fail to notice peaceful Balquhidder Glen, let alone find Kirkton Glen, with its entrance hidden in dense plantations. Yet Kirkton Glen to Glen Dochart is an ancient through-route, well-known to the clansmen and tenant farmers of former days. The lower slopes of the glen are completely muffled by mature plantations, in which the buzz of the forestry worker's saw

and the crash of trees can sometimes already be heard. Nevertheless, give the forest just over an hour of your time in each direction for the rewards of the uplands beyond the conifer belt; this walk is only worth doing if you are prepared to go all the way, out of the forest and on to the upper valley. It offers birdlife in plenty, great views north and south, a cliff of some botanical interest, a transparent lochan and superb rock scenery. Choose a sunny day, ideally, so you

can linger at the top of the pass. The route starts from Balquhidder Church, where many visitors stop at the grave of Rob Roy Macgregor. Note in passing that the gravestone is actually 14th-century - a Celtic stone, ancient even in Rob's day. The church itself, dated 1855, replaced an earlier series of religious buildings on this site, indicating the long history of settlement in this lovely green glen.

A Tiny goldcrests give the thinnest of squeakings from the tops of the Scots pine and larch. Look out for the larger (sparrow-sized) siskins, very handsome in green, black and yellow, which are common along this section.

B The first hint of a view, part of Meall an Fhiodhain, which you will ultimately stand under.

C The view begins to open out into an amphitheatre of uplands. Leave the primroses alone!

D The relief at your escape from the plantation, plus the short, sharp slope, will mean you will pause to look down the glen at this point. Note Stuc a' Chroin to the left of Ben Ledi, the two most prominent peaks.

E In this lonely spot, huge blocks have fallen from the hollowed-out face above. This area is popular with rock climbers, but our route leads safely round the base.

F On the left is the crystal-clear Lochan an Eireannaich - the little loch of the Irishman.

G Ben More is conspicuous westwards, sweeping up in a continuous rise from the main road running through Glen Dochart towards Crianlarich and the far west. There is a wide choice of 'Munros' -Ben Challum behind Crianlarich to the north-west, then, moving eastwards, Meall Glas and Sgiath Chuil are among the most identifiable of a complicated grouping of high hills, which are often known as the Mamlorn. From

this point, Meall nan Tarmachan and Ben Lawers are obscured by the shoulder of Meall an Fhiodhain.

H Observant walkers in April might note the low-growing cushions of purple saxifrage among the curiously eroded rocky hummocks. Many of Scotland's mountains are built of hard, acid rocks, such as quartzite or granite, with heather or crowberry dominant. But the widest variety of mountain plants prefer a basic rock like limestone or mica-schist. Remembering that Ben Lawers, famous for its mountain flora, lies only a little to the east, look out for a small cliffy outcrop below and to your right as you return, before you pass through the broken fence. Walkers interested in alpine plants might wish to divert for a few moments.

Over

12

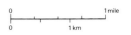

10 On the main path, go through a gap in the broken fence but do not lose height as the view opens out northwards. Skirt a little way round the slope on your right for your final viewpoint. Expect to take at least one and a half hours to reach this, your furthest point.

9 Walk on round the base of the rocks, north-westwards, until you rejoin the main path beyond the lochan.

8 In order to gain a close view of the magnificent rocks of Meall an Fhiodhain, the most spectacular crag on the right, veer left on the main path, but when below the middle craggy face, leave main path and cut right and up to the base of the jumble of huge rocks.

11 Retrace your steps a short way.

7 At last you break cover from the gloom and look out on to open uplands. Generations of walkers and sheep have made a selection of faint paths, the best of which veers a little left and upwards, heading towards the left-hand edge of the middle range of crags.

12 Turn right and go round the lochan, trying not to disturb the peeping sandpipers, and pick up the main path by the loch's outfall.

6 The track forks, with the left indicated as a forest walk and another notice pointing straight into the trees, bisecting the Y-junction. Take this middle path. You will have walked for at least an hour, unless very fit.

13 Follow the path back to the point in the forest where you emerged (point 7) and retrace your steps to Balquhidder.

5 All along this section, simply keep to the main track.

1 Park carefully in Balquhidder. There are some spaces just below the churchyard, signed to Rob Roy's grave. Walk through the churchyard, pausing to read a little of its history in the church porch, then turn right, round the side of the church.

4 At the clearly visible bridge on your left, continue upwards, keeping the main stream to your left. At time of writing, forestry operations had closed sections of the track on the far side anyway.

2 With the stream on the left below you, go through a gap in the wall and turn sharp right. Go over stile. The path becomes broader, twisting left and into the start of the tall conifers. At time of writing, the path was signed for Kirkton Glen Walks.

3 After about ten minutes walking, make sure you continue uphill, bearing slightly left on the main track. You will pass by the turning on the right for Craig an Tuirc, the viewpoint rock that overlooks the village.

Meall an Fhiodhain · 791

Lochan an Eireannaich

Kirkton Glen

Balquhidder   Church

Loch Voil

G E D C H F B A

0 ____ 1 mile
0 ____ 1 km

Walk 2
THE GLEN OGLE RAILWAY WALK
5 miles (8km) Easy, except for short steep section at start

This is a must for rail enthusiasts, as well as for groups looking for a flavour of the Highlands without too much of an element of risk. The route ascends Glen Ogle along the trackbed of the old Caledonian Railway which once ran north from Lochearnhead, then westwards, ultimately reaching Oban. The line was opened all the way to Oban in 1880 and finally closed in September 1965, a rockfall hastening the end of services which were already scheduled for closure later in the same year. Glen Ogle witnessed plenty of travellers in earlier centuries. The Romans are said to have passed this way, and so have armies, cattle drovers and royal visitors. By 1751, General Caulfield,

General Wade's successor, had completed this section of the Stirling to Fort William road. Portions of it are visible today: from the railway vantage-point look for the built-up banks on either side, characteristic of these early roads. This 18th-century communications network was a political necessity. Though the Glen Ogle road post-dates Culloden and the extinction of the Jacobite cause, a nervous government in far-off London still found it wise to garrison the Highlands, moving troops by specially-built roads.

Queen Victoria, viewing the scene from her horse-drawn carriage in September of 1842, remarked in her diary that the wildness reminded her of 'prints of the Kyber Pass' - and the

comparison is widely-quoted to this day. The upward journey is made easy by using the old railway trackbed, while the return is on a way-marked trail through a sheep-farm. The entire walk has been made possible through an access agreement between Stirling District Council and the landowner. **NOTE: Dogs are banned in the lambing season throughout March and April, and are not welcomed at any time. Keep them firmly on a lead and read the Introduction, section 7, for information on the rights of farmers under the Civic Government (Scotland) Act 1982.**

A Half-way up the field, while pausing for breath you will notice the old Lochearnhead Station, now converted to a Scout Centre. This lay on the old Crieff-Lochearnhead line, closed in 1951. The disparity in height between the two lines meant their junction was two miles further south at Balquhidder.

B At the ladder-stile giving access to the trackbed, the view down Loch Earn stretches eastwards. This was considered, in its day, the finest view from a train anywhere in Britain, nearly 800ft up on the hillside. The bulk of Ben Our obscures parts of Ben Vorlich, but its neighbour Stuc a' Chroin looks imposing.

C Note the Scots pine - which have seen the railway come and go. Also obvious are the scrubby birches meeting overhead. These young trees have grown up since the

railway disappeared. With the lineside fences originally in good order, sheep were excluded. The birches are a clear indication of the kind of tree regeneration which takes place when sheep are not present.

D At bridge 104, note the scar of a new access road on the hillside opposite. The railway would have been equally conspicuous when it was first pushed through. Between this bridge and the next, look for signs of the old military road, now a green track running near the burn.

E Between bridges 107 and 108, you will see evidence of the engineering problems: a rugged boulder-field above and left, that must have caused headaches for many a railway lengthman. A few scattered boulders on the trackbed in at least three places are slightly unsettling evidence of falls since the

railway closed. Just below the viaduct can be seen different generations of engineers' efforts to stabilise the rockwalls, originally with stone, later with brick (note the cement with the date 1946!).

F Before finally leaving the railway, note, beyond the cutting, the military road below again, though there is a confusing section of old main road above it. Caulfield's work is nearest the stream. Compare the old hump-backed bridge with the later old road bridge above it, nearer the main road, and think of the manpower that brought these communications through, when the main tools were gunpowder, picks and shovels.

G Across the road and on a little knoll, take time to look around at the wildness of the glen and the height of the railway opposite. *Over*

7 The top part of the path is faint but the general direction is clear, downhill between road and burn. You will eventually find a wide bit of old road, near the burn, probably a widened section of military road but now all grassed over.

6 Just beyond a footbridge, spanning a small section of trackbed that has disappeared, go right over ladder-stile and down to the little hump-backed bridge. You are on your return journey.

8 Note the alders growing in the stream bed. Cross a burn coming down from the left. The path then goes close to the road and crosses it beyond a ladder-stile. Watch for traffic.

9 Your return is by following the post-markers and climbing a succession of ladder-stiles, staying parallel with the road. You bypass some outbuildings on their upper side before eventually dropping to the tree-lined stream bank.

5 Take care on the viaduct: its left-hand parapet is missing in places, though the full width of the trackbed means you can cross in safety.

10 The Crieff-Lochearnhead railway viaduct is conspicuous as you approach the stream crossing. Go over the footbridge, then a ladder-stile and go through a gate near the electricity sub-station. You may be sharing this last field with photogenic Highland cattle, friendly enough at time of writing.

4 Turn right on trackbed.

11 Go over one last ladder-stile, on to main road and walk left, back into Lochearnhead.

3 Mount the steps on the upper side of the old station entrance drive and cross a ladder-stile. Your railway lies uphill and across the gorsy field.

2 Walk back to the junction, then right towards the dismantled rail bridge beside the viaduct. This is not the railway you will walk. Cross the main road and look for a sign 'Lochearnhead Scout Station', with a notice about the Glen Ogle trail.

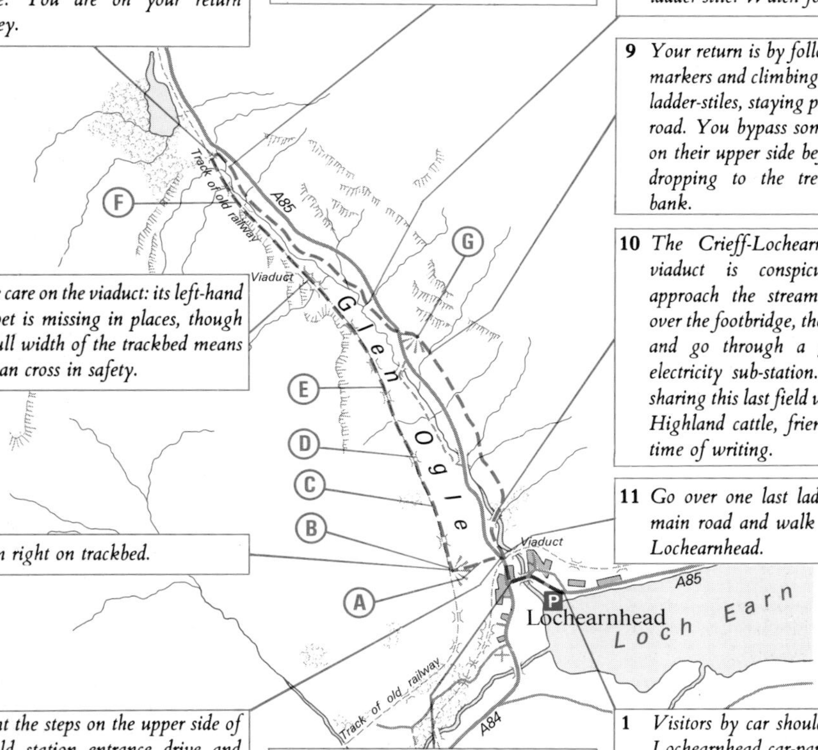

1 Visitors by car should use the main Lochearnhead car-park on the A85, by the loch-side, opposite the water sports centre.

Map labels: Track of old railway, A85, Viaduct, F, G, E, D, C, B, A, Glen Ogle, Viaduct, A85, Lochearnhead, P, Loch Earn, Track of old railway, A84

Walk 3
ABOVE THE PASS OF LENY
2 miles (3.5km) + 790ft (243m) Moderate; short strenuous sections

A walk with a surprising diversity of tree species and first-class views. If either your time or your lung-power is questionable, then the top can be omitted, making a mile walk with a rewarding view. Two contrasting landscapes can be enjoyed - south and east lie major population centres and intensive farming, north and west the mountain barriers begin to loom and stretch to the end of Scotland. Recommended as a summer evening walk.

5 *Path turns to the right. There are duckboards to assist the crossing of drainage channels. Shortly after, you must decide on Meall Garbh detour. It is the pine-covered little hill, the right-most of two which lie on your left. (The car park is otherwise only 10-15 minutes away, straight ahead then down right). Both options should be signposted.*

4 *Path makes its way uphill, before turning into a firebreak flanked by sitka spruce.*

3 *Go on through oaks along path notched into the hillside. At grove of Scots pine (the conifer with long needles all round the twig), the path turns sharply right.*

2 *The walk starts below the highest trees, at the back of the car park, midway between the two back parking areas and just to the left of a little gully. It may be signposted by the Forestry Commission and goes uphill parallel to the road and a little rocky underfoot. Douglas fir (note the flat needles) and cypress fringe this old charcoal burners' track.*

1 *Park in the car park signposted Falls of Leny. Coming west from Callander, the car park is right and set back from the road (although the Falls themselves are on the left of the road).*

6 *Meall Garbh paths plunges left through conifers then rises right and upwards through oak woods, heading towards the saddle between the two hills.*

7 *Rejoin the path, turning right and up, following the fence on the slope of Meall Garbh (translated as 'rough hill'). The path plunges back into the conifers, but if in doubt, the direction is unquestionably up. You will come back to the fence and the summit, but not before finding yourself on a little spur, with Meall nan Saighdear tree-covered and nearby on your right.*

8 *Descend by following the fence in the Callander direction at first. Take care on the short section of twisted heather and bracken before dropping right, into a tall conifer plantation.*

9 *Back into more pleasing woodland below; the path kinks on its descent. Look out for roe deer.*

10 *On reaching a small grove of stunted, overbrowsed conifers, the path is faint. Without gaining or losing height, go right to pick up a small stream. Turn left and down, following it back to the car park.*

A In season the oak woodland rings with birdsong. Look out for flattened areas once used for charcoal burning.

B This view makes it all worthwhile: Falls of Leny and road below, Callander to the south-east with the lowlands beyond.

C Through pine and larch can be seen the bulk of Ben Ledi to the west.

D Detour briefly left at the top of the saddle on the skyline for another magnificent view of Ben Ledi.

E On a clear day the summit view is as far as the Ochils to the east - and even the Pentlands beyond. Much nearer, the Menteith Hills are also conspicuous, as is Loch Lubnaig.

Walk 4

CALLANDER CRAGS

4 miles (6.5km) 890ft (273m) Mostly moderate

```
0                                  1 mile
|___|___|___|___|___|___|___|___|___|
0                     1 km
```

Callander Crags rise above Callander, looking almost inaccessible. Yet there are reasonable paths and rewarding views, far above the town. This walk also offers a diversion to the Bracklinn Falls, where Sir Walter Scott once rode his pony for a bet over the rickety bridge (now replaced!) that spans the Falls. Take care with children on the higher sections and at the Falls.

6 Continue eastwards keeping fence on left, losing height.

5 Continue along levelling path, noting steep path joining from right. Scramble across junction and follow fence on left to summit.

4 Cross small (and intermittent) stream and continue on.

3 Continue upwards with deer-proof fence on left.

2 Go left then follow path upwards. Path becomes steep and can be slippery. Keep conifers on right and beech trees on left. Follow a ruined wall upwards, also on left.

1 Park either in the large car park on the Crags side of the main street or on the road beside the tennis courts (Tulipan Crescent). Take path alongside tennis courts into woodland to Forestry Commission signpost.

7 With public road clearly in sight, go right, choosing path carefully over wet ground. Join road where signpost indicates route up. Turn right.

13 Cross bridge and continue past seat. A few minutes later tennis courts and your starting point come into view.

8 Fifteen minutes later, there is a sign to the Red Well, a chalybeate (iron-rich) spring only moments from the road.

9 At the Bracklinn Falls car park, turn left along clear path. Go through double kissing gate and down stepped path to view Falls. Return to car park.

10 Go down public road for about 100 yards (91m) till sign on right is reached, reading 'The Crags and Upper Wood Walk.' (N.B. This sign faces downhill, i.e. away from you). Turn right and go along this path. Do not lose height.

11 Go past fenced-off underground reservoir into thick woodland of larch, pine and deciduous trees. Path is now much improved and keeps on the level, crossing a number of small streamlets. Good place to see roe deer.

12 Path joins from right, by large oak tree, and drops sharply to left. Follow it left and down to green-railed bridge.

A After thick woodland and short rocky section, pause where path flattens out, for first views of town.

B First views of Ben Ledi, 2882ft (879m), north-westwards, and, to the south-east, Loch Venachar and the Menteith Hills.

C Good views over town from rocky ledge. Note St Kessog's Church, below, and the River Teith.

D From the Queen Victoria Jubilee Cairn, there is a complete panorama: Ben Vorlich and Stuc a' Chroin northwards and (clockwise) Dumyat in the Ochils, the Wallace Monument and Stirling Castle, the Forth valley as far as the Pentlands, the Fintry Hills, the Menteith Hills, Ben Venue, Ben Ledi.

E View from the bridge of spectacular Falls and mature mixed woodland of oak, ash and alder.

Walk 5
BEN LEDI
6 miles (9.5km) + 2450ft (750m) Strenuous; attempt ONLY in fine weather

Unlike most of the comparatively low-lying walks in this book, Ben Ledi presents a challenge to all but the habitual Scottish hillwalker. Unless the party is well-shod, carrying spare clothing, waterproofs, adequate reserve food, a compass and an additional map (OS 1:50 000 Sheet 57) do not attempt this walk. Equally, because this is a high-level walk, **attempt it only in fine weather**. There are dangerous slopes to the east, particularly if late snow is still lying. To mitigate the cautious note, the Forestry Com-

mission have waymarked most of the route, though posts and markers have an odd habit of disappearing at these higher altitudes. It is a splendid day out, with rewarding views in all directions, particularly as Ben Ledi lies right on the edge of the Highlands and is a conspicuous landmark not just for the browsers on Callander Main Street, but also from many parts of the eastern lowlands, including the ramparts of Edinburgh Castle. The first part of the ascent climbs steeply through plantations to gain the far southern

edge of the eventual summit plateau, bypassing the steep eastern face. From the summit the path leads down to the Bealach nan Corp, the rather ghoulishly-named Pass of the Bodies. Nearby is Lochan nan Corp, where a funeral party, crossing in dead of winter, so to speak, once fell through the ice. Suitably cheered, you then drop into the lovely but unfortunately-named Stank Glen and return through dense forest to the level reaches of an old railway.

10 The summit route resolves itself as a broad grassy ridge, easy underfoot. Eventually, even the bilberry becomes dwarf then disappears. Most of the hard climbing has been done on the lower parts of the route; it is time instead to enjoy the splendid views.

9 The path follows a broken line of iron fence-posts, a handy marker should cloud descend unexpectedly (in which case, abandon the walk and return by the way you have come).

8 The path finally and clearly turns right, with a view opening out south-westwards. There is a cairn.

7 Be prepared to walk a surprisingly long way upwards and left to avoid all the crags. Do not be tempted by any shortcuts to the right.

6 Go over the stream, cross a newish fence by a stile and bear left and up; the path is fairly conspicuous.

5 The woodland drops away; check that you have a stream on your right and the rocky face of Ledi ahead.

1 To reach the starting point from the Callander direction, go past the first Falls of Leny car park. Less than a mile further on, as the Pass of Leny opens out, take a sharp left turn over a bridge on to the old railway trackbed. Park opposite or left again.

2 The path leads up from a deer-proof kissing-gate, immediately beyond the bridge.

3 A relentless ascent, a bit steep and rocky; walking boots essential.

4 Note the change to Douglas fir (flat needles, whitish beneath) where the path momentarily levels off. Above the clearing, where the path swings up to the right, look for Stirling Castle, behind you, to the east.

Over

18

13 *At the Bealach nan Corp, at time of writing, a wooden post indicates where you should turn sharply right and down, starting at the source of a little stream, which you then follow. The path should be waymarked all the way down to a fence, with the stream on your left.*

14 *An odd diversion, courtesy of the Forestry Commission. Go right, not through the gate, then go on beside the fence. You will even have to go up a little. The path is now wet and slippery on the heather-roots. Keep the fence on your left.*

15 *Look for a stile, just before the high trees start. Go left over it and down.*

16 *At main track, go right and follow it down into the dense conifers.*

17 *You reach a newish road, built for timber extraction. Turn right on to it, then almost immediately take a waymarked path going down left.*

12 *Look for the fence-posts changing direction to the north-west, that is, away from your expected route home. Follow them to ensure that you turn all the crags below, while at the same time aiming for the lowest point of the pass. If cloud descends, you must trust these fence-posts and not cut corners by turning right and steeply down too soon.*

18 *Reaching a U-bend in the forestry road, the path is waymarked to continue left, to the waterside. There are steep drops on the left of this path and an alternative for tired legs would be to follow the forestry road down. The suggested path joins it anyway, lower down.*

11 *Now follow the continuing line of fence-posts descending northwards on the ridge which narrows a little. Beware of the corrie, with its steep headwall, on your immediate right as you descend. Do not attempt to lose height any other way than by letting the safest part of the ridge with its fence-posts take you gradually down.*

19 *Follow the forestry road down but join the old railway, now a surfaced road, at the first opportunity, going right and back to the car park.*

A The old military road from Stirling to Fort William, (see Walk 2, Glen Ogle) can be traced among the trees on the other side of the valley.

B Botanists will note, in season, a variety of plant life on this section. Alpine Lady's Mantle, with its deeply-lobed, five-fingered leaf, silvery below, overlaps with the 'ordinary' variety, much less deeply cut. Crowberry is also widespread.

C As you ascend, first The Cobbler, craggy, on the far horizon, then the rest of the Arrochar Hills begin to appear. Loch Venachar is also conspicuous in the foreground.

D From the summit, not unexpectedly, there is a splendid panorama, lowland and Highland with the very best of Argyll and Perthshire's mountains to be seen. Not too far away are Ben Vorlich and Stuc a' Chroin, north-eastwards across the valley, while the giants above Balquhidder, Ben More and Stobinian, hold snow till late in the season. (On midsummer night the sun goes down between them, as seen from this point.) Note how oddly inconspicuous Ben Lomond seems, as it hides behind a nearer but smaller Ben Venue. Loch Arklet gleams distantly in the west.

E Pause here to appreciate the wildness of the view from the upper part of the Stank Glen. Below you and disappearing in the trees are the ruins of old sheilings, a reminder of a vanished way of life when women and children migrated to the upland pastures for the summer, to graze the cattle, leaving the lower farms for crop-growing.

F At this point look up to the rock pinnacles to appreciate the concern to keep you on high ground till the bealach was reached!

G Note the waterfall.

Walk 6
AROUND CALLANDER
4.5 miles (7.5km) Mostly easy, some rough walking in woodland

Though the woods behind Callander and its crags (Walk 4) are the most popular, they are not the only walking area in the immediate environs of this popular centre. This walk combines woodland paths, roads and the old Callander and Oban Railway - which you meet on other walks - to give a circular route from which the setting of the town can be appreciated, as well as something of the history of the area. On the railway walkway, you pass near the hamlet of Kilmahog (the 'Kil' prefix usually means a cell or church - in this case of the little-known St Chug) which has been associated with the woollen industry for centuries. Water-power enabled local manufacture to take place (the Kilmahog Woollen Mill has preserved its water wheel) while the area has the slightly dubious distinction of being one of the very first in Scotland to introduce the black-faced sheep in the 18th century. You also pass near the dam of Loch Venachar, constructed at the same time as the main Loch Katrine works in 1859, and walk by the ancient Caledonian defensive position of Dunmore Hill. The walk even boasts a Roman camp, though the builders of the Callander and Oban Railway built an embankment across it. While the first part of the route is not a very severe test of navigation, if you do want to keep to schedule and find your way efficiently through to the Coilhallan Wood car park and hence the road, please follow the woodland instructions closely.

A This path, known hereabouts as 'the Mollands', from a nearby farm name, leads on to a network of woodland walks, well-known to local inhabitants.

B Note views of twin hills opposite: the left is the site of Dunmore Fort; the right, Bochastle Hill, has a large boulder, an 'erratic', dumped by a glacier 10,000 years ago, known as Samson's Putting Stone.

C The Eas Gobhain supplies compensation water to the River Forth via the River Teith (the confluence is just at the car park, your starting point). The masonry dam upstream from this point has eleven sluices and two salmon ladders for regulating the compensation water. There are views of Loch Venachar on your left and at this point you may or may not be sampling the 68.5 inches (1740mm) of rainfall which give the Trossachs their fresh appearance. (Loch Katrine gets 16 inches more!)

D The ancient ramparts of Dunmore Fort are not at their most conspicuous as you look upwards, left. The steep slope facing you afforded the ancient Caledonian settlers natural protection to the east.

E Orchids, water avens (down-turned wine-coloured heads) and orange hawkweed (a handsome bright red-orange up-market dandelion also known as 'foxes and cubs') have quickly colonised the trackbed. Listen for curlews in the fields. A view of the hamlet of Kilmahog appears to the left.

F The Roman camp can only be recognised by a low ridge at right-angles to the railway on your left. This 1st-century AD camp is adjacent to an earlier temporary camp of a kind unique to Scotland; only ten examples have been found. Remember that you are north of the Antonine Wall and looking at evidence of a campaign of subjugation that never wholly succeeded. The camp is significantly sited by the Pass of Leny, an ancient through-route to the north.

Over

16 Follow the trackbed over the bridge, then go right, through the well-kept park, heading roughly for the church spire, to reach the car park.

15 At sign to picnic area, cross the main road with care and go right on to the walkway adjacent to the picnic area. This follows the railway trackbed which goes under the old road-bridge. Continue along for approximately 1.25 miles (2km).

14 At the junction of the main Trossachs road, go right. There is a footpath/pavement on the north (left-hand) side of this short but sometimes busy tourist road.

13 There are no pavements along this next short section, so take care. Turn right at the junction over the bridge, signed A821 Trossachs.

12 When you emerge from the path on to a forestry road, go left. You should be in the Coilhallan Wood car park, which has other Forestry Commission walks. Go left along the tarred road beyond the car park.

11 After a clearing in the trees above you, the path begins to drop right, becoming clearer, in a direction a little to the north of west.

10 At the first firebreak split, shortly after you start walking along it, keep on path ahead and do not go right. Continue along the main break, which becomes very rutted.

1 Though there are other car parks, if travelling west, it is suggested that you park near the centre of Callander by taking the next left after the road signed for the A81 which goes across the river. Your car park is on the river side, behind the Caledonian Hotel. Park and make your way left, along the river bank and through the children's playground (noting the children's slide irreverently decorating the ancient mound of Tom ma Chisaig). You reach the A81 through a gap in the wall. Go right and cross the bridge.

9 Your way is blocked by a fence and another wall running in at right angles to your original wall. Go right over broken down section of wall and down, under a large beech tree, then on to the firebreak about 30 yards (27 m) away. Go left along it, on a faint path.

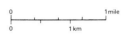

2 As the main road swings left, cross over a minor road going off right and continue on. Look for a wood starting on the right and immediately after it, a gap in the wall on the right, with two stone pillars. (N.B. If you reach the large school on the left, then you have overshot.) Go right between pillars and on to path.

3 The path goes uphill through pleasant woodland.

4 Go through kissing gate, staying on main path, going slightly left and uphill.

5 Keep straight on at next fork, staying near the wood edge. Do not go right yet.

6 An important location to find: where the woodland thickens on your left, look for another fork, with an old wall leading off right. Go right down this path, heading more deeply into the woods with the wall on your right.

7 Make your way past (round, over or through) the fallen rowan that blocks the path.

8 Another critical navigation check: the first wall meets a second at an angle, about 50 yards (46 m) beyond the shattered tree. Continue ahead on path.

FALLS OF LENY
2 miles (3.5km) with optional 3 mile (5km) extension Easy

The Falls of Leny are often visited from the north (or main A84 side) from a nearby car park (used in Walk 3, Above the Pass of Leny). However, this delightful stroll visits them courtesy of the Cailander-Oban Railway, the closure of which is much lamented. There are oak woods and wild water, birds and flowers to see in this short expedition. Take care with children, should one divert to the edge of the Falls. The extension suggested is a there-and-back-again walk eastwards towards Callander, and will interest birdwatchers in particular.

The track bed of the former railway is now an improved cycleway, part of a route from Glasgow via the Trossachs, and the walking is easy underfoot, with bridges and ramps making the Bridgend Cottage to Ben Ledi car park section suitable for pushchairs/wheelchairs.

3 *Make the most of this delightful level path and enjoy the bird-song in season and the cow-wheat, creeping jenny, violets and many other plants. The river at this point is called the Garbh Uisge, the 'rough water'.*

2 *Leave the car park on the ramp at the parapet of the dismantled bridge. There is a path here, which is very well maintained and easy to follow. Follow this downstream.*

1 *Of the two car parks used to visit the Falls, this is the second. If coming from Callander you will see one on the right first. Go past it for less than a mile. As the Pass of Leny opens out, take a sharp left turn over a bridge on to the track bed. The car park is left again along the old railway. Park at the far end, near the parapet of the dismantled bridge.*

4 *The sheltered, upgraded path, which is very easy to follow, runs through attractive oak woodland.*

5 *Rejoin the railway embankment near a second dismantled bridge. The falls are a little way downstream.*

6 *About 100 yards (91m) after the bridges mentioned at point C, exploratory visitors have made a path, left, to the Falls; go through the wire and follow it down.*

10 *Retrace your steps along the trackbed, going straight ahead at the small bridge mentioned in point 8 and following outward path (left) at bridge parapet.*

7 *Follow the path to the bank, then downstream. It is faint in places, but continue beside the water's edge until the path becomes clearer again, winding up through the trees, back to the railway.*

8 *Having rejoined the railway at a small bridge, decide if you wish to retrace your steps or continue towards Kilmahog. It is about half an hour back to the car park from this point, if you turn right, back along the track bed to the parapet (point C), then go left and retrace your steps.*

9 *If you wish to lengthen the walk, go left. The path eventually meets the A821 (after about 30 minutes' walk) and this road makes a convenient turning point.*

A Over the parapet of the dismantled bridge, look for grey wagtails, dippers and kingfishers.

B Corriechrombie, the 'bent birch corrie' is an old settlement upstream. Now upgraded to form a cycle and walking route, the path closely follows the old track which linked it with Callander and which pre-dates the military road and the railway.

C From the old parapet, looking north, note how the railway builders were forced to construct two bridges close together because of the difficult terrain, which has also squeezed the road and river together. Ben Ledi (Walk 5) is ahead and the old charcoal burners' path (Walk 3) is in the trees opposite and right.

D Note from the Falls the conspicuous and made-up path used by the less adventurous visitors on the far bank. Take care with small children; the bank here is steep.

Walk 8
THE MENTEITH HILLS
4 miles (6.5km) at least   Easy

The Highland Boundary Fault not only cuts across Loch Lomond. It also runs through Loch Venachar. Thus walkers on this path up the south side of Venachar are really in the beginnings of the lowlands, looking northwards into splendid Highland scenery. The path goes through recent conifer plantings then out into a moorland bowl, hemmed in by mini-crags to the north. Try it for an evening's ramble, to watch the sunset, giving the walk a couple of hours at least.

This there-and-back route has been included to give you the option of doing as much or as little as you like. Even walking boots are not essential, though (as ever) preferable.

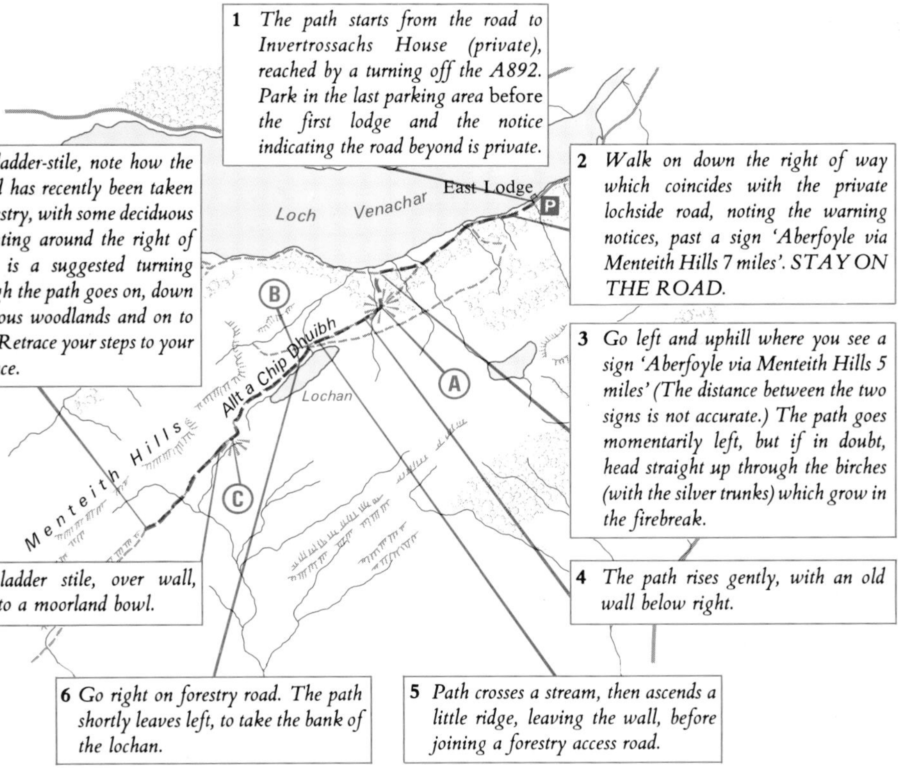

1 The path starts from the road to Invertrossachs House (private), reached by a turning off the A892. Park in the last parking area before the first lodge and the notice indicating the road beyond is private.

8 At second ladder-stile, note how the area beyond has recently been taken over for forestry, with some deciduous shelter planting around the right of way. This is a suggested turning point, though the path goes on, down into coniferous woodlands and on to Aberfoyle. Retrace your steps to your parking place.

2 Walk on down the right of way which coincides with the private lochside road, noting the warning notices, past a sign 'Aberfoyle via Menteith Hills 7 miles'. STAY ON THE ROAD.

3 Go left and uphill where you see a sign 'Aberfoyle via Menteith Hills 5 miles' (The distance between the two signs is not accurate.) The path goes momentarily left, but if in doubt, head straight up through the birches (with the silver trunks) which grow in the firebreak.

4 The path rises gently, with an old wall below right.

7 Go over ladder stile, over wall, opening into a moorland bowl.

6 Go right on forestry road. The path shortly leaves left, to take the bank of the lochan.

5 Path crosses a stream, then ascends a little ridge, leaving the wall, before joining a forestry access road.

(map labels: East Lodge, Loch Venachar, Allt a Chip Dhuibh, Lochan, Menteith Hills, B, A, C, P)

A Callander is seen eastwards on the right. Loch Venachar lies below and there is an end-on view of Ben Ledi. Further west, Ben An (Walk 17) looms over the Trossachs gateway. Ben Venue is already beginning to disappear behind a nearby shoulder.

B Note the sheep pens below, disappearing in the young trees. There is a lochan here, too, presumably formed by the damming of a marshy area by the forestry road.

C A viewpoint southwards, Dumgoyne is the conspicuous hump on the edge of the Campsies.

Walk 9

GARTMORN DAM AND FOREST MILL
3 miles (5 km) with optional 3 mile (5 km) extension   Easy

The northern side of the Forth Valley may give the initial impression of being despoiled in places by a variety of industries and mineworkings past and present. But this is quite inaccurate. Gartmorn Dam may owe its origins to 18th-century enterprise - its stored waters once drove mine pumping machinery, as well as seven mills in Alloa - but now this substantial loch is a nature reserve with extensive woodlands, particularly at its eastern end. This walk is for nature lovers - plenty of wildlife, plus a varied habitat on the Forest Mill optional there-and-back section, with red and grey squirrels' distribution, rather unusually, overlapping. A leisurely outing for all ages, with the ramparts of the Ochils looming to the north.

1 Park as indicated by notices on the lochside, having followed signs from Alloa on the A908. Make your way anticlockwise, round to the right on the embankment. Pass the Visitor Centre.

2 Go left on signposted path, just before warden's cottage.

3 Path briefly splits; take right fork on to embankment and leave the lochside.

4 At stile at water's edge, turn right to follow bank.

5 Continue to follow bank path, bearing left.

6 Shortly after sign to Coalsnaughton, cross bridge and turn immediately right through gap in fence, should you wish to take the diversion to Forest Mill. The route is scenic, but the turning point less so. Allow about 40 minutes to reach Forest Mill (N.B. There is no mill now to be seen.) Otherwise, continue from point 11.

7 Follow feeder stream on north bank, then cross bridge and continue upstream, now in pleasant woodland.

8 The artificial nature of this stream becomes apparent. The River Black Devon rushes below. Take care to keep on the embankment. Continue on main path.

9 Path eventually joins field access road at Aitkenhead Farm. Keep on stream bank, noting variety of woodland.

10 As you near the A977 at Forest Mill, retrace your steps to bridge mentioned at point 6.

11 Continue to follow original path to right, past red pantile-roofed house, away briefly from the dam.

12 The path going left and back to the dam is signposted after the small stream.

13 Follow path back to car park.

A Viewpoint from high bank. With binoculars, look out for mallard, wigeon, teal, pochard, tufted duck, great crested grebe - among the commoner species.

B A little knoll that gives a long panorama of the dam. Dumyat is the prominent hill furthest to the west along the line of the Ochils to the north. Allow 45 minutes from the car park, assuming ornithological stops.

C Good birdwatching spot behind screens on path.

Coalsnaughton
B140
New Sauchie
Gartmorn Dam
Aitkenhead
Forest Mill
Black Devon
Clackmannan
B910
A907
A977
A908

Walk 10

DUMYAT

3 miles (5km) + 700ft (218m) Easy/moderate

Gaining its name, some authorities say, from the fortresss of the Maeatae (Dun Maeatae), an ancient Pictish tribe, this hill may be lower than some of its more easterly neighbours in the Ochils, but its distinct dome makes it a landmark overlooking the Forth Valley. It is a popular walk for its extensive views. You are strongly advised to choose a clear day. A public road enables the car-borne visitor to gain height easily, before reaching the car park. The temptation to come off the hill in a north-westerly direction and head towards a road and reservoir for a roundabout return should be resisted as this is not on any right of way. **Keep your dog under strict control and on a lead - this is sheep country.** (N.B. The name is pronounced 'Dim-aye-at' with the emphasis on the middle syllable.)

1 *From the Stirling to Bridge of Allan road, the A9(T), follow signs to Sheriffmuir, on the Bridge of Allan side of Stirling University campus. The road twists uphill until open moorland is reached. There is a car park on the right, near a pylon. At time of writing, a footpath sign directs you to a stile. Go over it and head eastwards.*

2 *The path splits almost immediately, though the left fork is faint. Continue on the level, taking the right fork.*

8 *At its right-hand or western side, look for a path running off right which keeps to higher ground than the ascent path. Follow it till it rejoins the outward route at point 2, with the car park only a few yards further on.*

Dumyat

Ⓐ

Ⓑ

Ⓒ

Ⓓ

Fort ∴ △ Cairn
Castle Law

3 *Another path wanders off to the right, towards the trees. Ignore it.*

7 *Retrace your steps to the back of the knoll mentioned at point 4.*

4 *Near signs of an old sheepfold (on the right) the path goes left and upwards, then gives a choice of up or round a heathery knoll.*

5 *After the first boggy stream, keep steeply rising ground on left. Path points straight to the summit.*

6 *Cross fence, or take left fork to stile to avoid boggy ground. The path is momentarily steep and rocky on its short pull to the top.*

A Below and southwards are Stirling Castle and the Wallace Monument - already the views are extensive.

B Note the two summits ahead. Left is Dumyat, right is Castle Law, the actual site of the fort.

C A momentary digression left will give a view of the ancient remains of the Castle Law fort. Two ruined walls are conspicuous (but flattened). The inner enclosure is thought to be later than these outer walls.

D The Cleish Hills are far off to the east, the Pentlands are beyond the Forth Valley, but the views to the Trossachs hills are the most spectacular, with Ben Ledi, Ben Venue and Ben Lomond prominent.

BEN CLEUCH

6.5 miles (10.5km) + 2,200ft (671m)   Moderate; some difficult places; walk only in fine weather

The eroded rocks that are actually ancient lava flows give the Ochils, east of Stirling, a rounded, grassy appearance, behind their impressive scarp face. However, the sheep-nibbled turf can tilt alarmingly into steep-sided valleys; one of them holds the start of this route to the top of the highest of the Ochils. Ben Cleuch, for altitude and view, can hold its head as high as many of the Trossachs hills. **This is one of the highest walks in the book, requiring good footwear, proper clothing,** **refreshments, a compass and an additional map - OS 1:50 000 Sheet 58. The walk should only be attempted in good weather.** As everywhere else in the Ochils, it is sheep country and **dogs are not advised**. If you travel from the south, say, over the Kincardine Bridge, as you approach Tillicoultry, your starting point, look for the highest part of the Ochils ahead. The summit of Ben Cleuch is at the centre of a long whaleback, and its eastern shoulder, The Law, is where the steep ascent levels off. Note that this (first) top has a cairn, a useful navigational aid should cloud descend. The route goes along the skyline and drops eventually into the Silver Glen, where Sir John Erskine of Alva Estate mined silver in the early 18th century. The return along the face of the hills runs through this same estate, now the Ochil Hills Woodland Park, giving easy walking for tired limbs on the homeward stretch.

5 *There is no option here but the long pull to the summit-cairn of The Law, noting, between puffs, the woodrush, a strap-leafed plant that indicates this open windy space was once wooded.*

6 *As you near the summit cairn of The Law, note the fence running in from the right.*

1 *Turn left off the main A91 immediately after entering Tillicoultry from the west. Parallel with a burn immediately to the left, the road runs uphill until a park is seen, hard against the face of the Ochil Hills. If the small parking area here (near the toilets) is full, then park by the burn a little way down the hill. The park is the entrance to the Mill Glen.*

4 *At the highest point, after the path crosses back to bring the burn on your left, the handrail ends and the path doubles back up. This is near the meeting point of the Daiglen and Gannel Burns. Do not follow this path any further. Ahead and on your left, as you look over the handrail, should be visible a path going between some rocky outcrops on the far bank and up the shoulder of The Law, that is, the hill between the two valleys. Reach this path by dropping down carefully to the waterside and crossing a small wooden bridge.*

3 *Make sure you go right after this (fifth) bridge, avoiding a zig-zagging track going off left.*

2 *Rather unexpectedly, the Mill Glen has a 'proper' pathway and bridges all the way to the junction of the Daiglen and Gannel Burns. Try to ignore in the lower stretch the fact that it is at one point no more than a few yards from a yawning quarry, supplying road-building material. Take care of children.*

Map labels: Ben Cleuch, The Law, The Nebit, Glentanner Burn, Silver Glen, Silver Burn, Daiglen Burn, Mill Glen, Gannel Burn, Waterfall, Waterfalls, Golf Course, Alva, Tillicoultry, A91, B, C, D, E, A, P

Over

0   1 mile
0   1 km

9 About half a mile (a kilometre) west of and 450ft (137m) below the summit, the path crosses a fence running north-south which meets the fence which has been on your right since The Law. Continue west down very steep slopes to reach the Glenwinnel Burn track.

10 Go left at the track and continue on for 1.5 miles (2.5km), passing through gate towards the end, shortly before track begins to zig-zag downhill.

11 The track zig-zags down the face of the hill. At the third bend on the eastern side, look for a gate going off into the larches. Go through it and continue on to cross the Silver Burn. (Note: if uncertain exactly where to enter the woodland, as you reach the zig-zag section, look down to where two sycamore trees grow close together on the edge of the field. This marks the gated entry point.)

8 To descend, follow the path westwards — the direction is important if visibility is poor — taking care if grass is wet on slightly steeper section.

12 Look for the main estate car park on the right as you near the foot of the slope. Join metalled road which gives access to a hotel. Take care with traffic as you emerge here. Go left.

13 Go past hotel keeping on main track, which eventually emerges close to golf course. Look out for that dangerous species, the erratic golfer, to be found sometimes on your right.

7 The path to the summit roughly follows the fence and should be obvious enough from the top of The Law. In bad visibility (in which … unless you are experienced, you … not to be here), you will find … is a useful marker.

14 Cross quarry access road, keeping on an easterly course turning right briefly on to it then picking up a short track that joins houses again by a street called Shillinghill. Ahead you will see the burn and car park.

… used dam, which you find … you cross the fifth … once supplied water to … ill.

… summit indicator … stunning panorama … day encompasses … rdeenshire, the … s Rock in East … l on Arran.

C The Silver Burn, with its old silver workings, is below, left.

D Sycamore woodland, prolifically seeding itself hereabouts, is less rich in birdsong than the oak woods encountered elsewhere. Sycamore, a non-native tree, plays host to a much smaller range of insects than the native oak. However, listen for the laughing call of the green

woodpecker as well as the call of the carrion crow, sounding like an old-fashioned motor car horn or klaxon, from the heights above you.

E On your left, the Adam stable block, all that remains of Alva House, is now a hotel, visitor centre and craft shop.

Ben Cleuch

The Law

The Nebit

Glenwinnel Burn

Daiglen Burn

Gannel Burn

Silver Glen

Silver Burn

Mill Glen

Waterfall

Waterfalls

The Nebit

Alva

Tillicoultry

Golf Course

A91

A SCRAMBLE IN THE OCHILS

3 miles (5km)   Moderate, difficult in places; some steep drops

The Ochils provide a foretaste of the Highlands and at the same time command respect. Grassy slopes can be steep and slippery. This walk, particularly the second part through Alva Glen, is definitely not for vertigo sufferers - it is also **UNSUITABLE FOR SMALL CHILDREN**. The descent to Alva Glen from the Glenwinnel Burn demands great care, while the glen itself has a number of scenically spectacular drops into the stream below. This little expedition offers a couple of hours on the hill for adventurous and responsible walkers, offering good views across the Forth Valley and the windy wide-open spaces of the Ochils. In case you find the scale of these hills confusing, remember that this walk is essentially a route round the hill called The Nebit. N.B. **Keep dogs on leads please**.

Parking: from the A91 east of Alva, look for signs to the Ochil Hills Woodland Park and take the road parallel to it, towards the hills. Go past the cemetery. Turn right, again, towards the hills, just before the new housing estate and park in small parking area.

A Look behind to the Forth Valley. The conspicuous storage sheds are DCL bonded warehouses. Away to the right, westwards, is the Wallace Monument.

B Waterfall viewpoint on little knoll, on the path described at point 9.

C At water works, note architecture of Strude Mill, built 1828, glimpsed through trees on right.

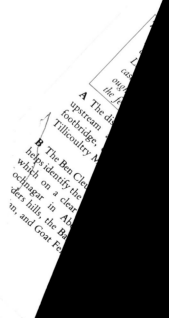

8 Cross the stream where it narrows below the main fall. **TAKE CARE HERE** - there is a second shorter fall below you. Now drop down to the main stream in the glen. Turn momentarily right to cross upstream, your spot dependent on water level.

7 Alva Glen is straight ahead but **TAKE CARE**. A sheep-track will take you away from the edge of the burn and above a makeshift bridge that marks the top of the waterfall. Look for the dark rock of the top of the waterfall, but keep it well away on your right. **DESCEND CAREFULLY** on the edge of the waterfall bowl, through the bracken to a lower level.

6 At the burn, turn left and downstream, following sheeptrack.

9 Ascend to path on west, or right-hand side of Alva Glen, looking downstream. Turn left and downstream.

5 At the junction of these two tracks, go off half-left and north-westwards to drop down to the Glenwinnel Burn. (N.B. if you overshoot this point, you will see the Glenwinnel Burn from the continuation of the main path. The further you go, the less steep is the descent to the burn). Note that The Nebit, which has a fence round it, is still high on your left.

10 Taking care on steep path, reach handrail over rocky section where path is momentarily faint.

11 Look for a dam left, below you. There is a steep zig-zag descent to it.

12 Cross bridge beside dam waterfall, the first of three on well-constructed unmistakable path, some of it handrailed.

4 Go through the gate and continue walking gently uphill for ABOUT 15 MINUTES. Look for a short track that joins from the right. Your path has levelled on a marshy watershed at this point.

13 Continue down to car park.

Alva Glen *Waterfall* Glenwinnel *Burn* *Waterfall* The Nebit Silver Burn (B) *Waterfall* Alva Burn Reservoir *Dam* *Waterfall* (A) (C) *Waterfall* Waterfalls *Water Works* (P) Alva A91

1 The path can be seen going diagonally upwards, above a bulldozed access track, east of Alva Glen itself. Walk uphill from parking area. The road swings left past a single pair of semi-detached houses. Go immediately right and up to reach water works.

2 Take right fork where track circles round square building and look for pedestrians-only gate in trees on right. Go through it and strike steeply uphill along brackeny path and sheep-cropped turf, slippery when wet.

3 Path joins track hairpinning its way uphill. Continue uphill on track. The Nebit is the hill immediately rising to your left.

Walk 13
THE DARN ROAD
4 miles (6.5km)   Easy

This ancient way could have been the main road northwards in the early Christian era - armed Roman legions perhaps passed along it. Linking Dunblane and Bridge of Allan, it leads the visitor away from the hubbub of the A9 and through pleasantly wooded parkland, to a landscape woven into Robert Louis Stevenson's *Kidnapped*. Small children should be watched on the banks of the Allan Water, and the Cock's Burn's gully needs a little respect.

3 *Path goes through gate with estate boundary wall on right and fence on left. Kippenross House is ahead, beyond the wall.*

2 *Return to dual carriageway and cross carefully to join path. Look for signpost 'Footpath to Bridge of Allan 3 Miles' and information board. Go through kissing gate and straight on.*

1 *Take last exit on left (just before roundabout at end of dual carriageway) while driving northwards along the A9 on the edge of Dunblane. Car park is (signed) downhill then left and right.*

4 *Path continues in sheltered dip with walls on each side.*

5 *Woodland on either side. The path runs under yews and drops to the Wharry Burn.*

6 *Go over footbridge and right to the banks of the Allan Water and downstream.*

7 *Shortly after Allan Water footbridge (do not cross) Stevenson's Cave (associated with the author R.L. Stevenson), appears on left. Immediately after, take path left on to higher level of steepening bank.*

12 *Return to Darn Road at noticeboard at Wharry Burn, an easy hour after you left it. Retrace your path, over the footbridge, up and under the yews and on to Dunblane.*

11 *At road go left. Pass road merging from right, then shortly go left again down track with white gate (propped open) at its start. Go straight on at hilltop on to a track leading down, NOT into private driveway to Drumdruills on right.*

8 *The gully of the Cock's Burn is crossed by a small footbridge. Turn right to regain Darn Road for a 10 minute excursion downstream.*

9 *Continue downstream to old weir and fish ladder. The paper mills are now a caravan site. Then retrace your steps as far as Cock's Burn.*

10 *Do not recross small footbridge. Go right and upstream to the public road.*

A Viewpoint at next information board: glimpses of the Trossachs hills on right and Gargunnock hills southwards across the parkland of Kippenross House.

B Look out for houses of Bridge of Allan and Stirling Castle appearing beyond the trees ahead.

C Note giant redwood tree in plantation on left.

D This viewpoint overlooks the Ladies' Pool, scene of a drowning accident in 1832. The Stirling Plain is southwards and the Victorian mansions of Bridge of Allan, built in its boom years as a spa, begin to appear to the south-east.

E View southwards over woodland to the Stirling Plain.

30

Walk 14
AROUND DOON HILL
2 miles (3.5km)   Easy

Doon Hill is associated with the 17th-century Gaelic scholar, the Reverend Robert Kirk, who investigated local fairy lore and published *The Secret Commonwealth* in 1691. As punishment for giving away the secrets of this Scottish supernatural world, he is said to have been spirited away to fairyland while walking on either this hill or Fairy Knowe nearby. The pine tree at the summit of this walk is said to contain the spirit of the minister. Evidence of 'the little folk' may be hard to find today, but evidence of part of the route is much simpler. Out of all the walks in this book, none is so clearly marked for part of the way as this one. Follow the toadstool signs, definitely not made by the fairies. Beautiful oaks, lots of birdsong - an evening stroll in enchanted woodland, all within easy reach of Aberfoyle (and, for this part of the country, Doon is a very small hill!).

2 *Aberfoyle is on the left across the low river-meadows. Look for sign on right pointing to path left into wood. Take this clearly marked path, which goes uphill and right, eventually through short coniferous belt.*

1 *If driving west, immediately after the junction of the B829, to Stronachlachar, with the A821 (Duke's Road) in Aberfoyle, turn left over a bridge and continue southwards to find Forestry Commission Balleich parking place. A number of waymarked routes start from this point, but follow Doon Hill signs on the surfaced road, left.*

8 *Return to car by turning right on main forestry track.*

3 *The summit views are restricted by the leafy canopy, but the birdlife is varied. The route down heads off northwards.*

4 *As the path heads into larches, look right and down for the track that circles this part of the hill. Drop down to it and turn right.*

5 *The wide track fades away here, replaced by a vague footpath. If in doubt follow the base of the hill, now looking unexpectedly tall on the right.*

6 *Path faint among the coppiced oaks; continue more or less straight ahead on the level and do not take path that rises on right. Leave well alone the primroses that grow on the south-facing bank.*

7 *Path suddenly rejoins the trail with its toadstool signs. Turn left and down, enjoying the honeysuckle scent in season.*

A Note the bilberry and holly growing abundantly in the shelter of the oaks.

B You have now left the waymarked route; to the left is birch with marshy meadows beyond while oaks cover the hill above and right. In spring listen hereabouts for snipe 'drumming' - making a strange resonant bleating sound with their specially-stiffened tail feathers held out against the air currents as they make their display flights. This difficult-to-locate noise carries a long way and is hard to relate to a high-flying small bird. Listen for chiffchaffs repeating their own names in the oaks on the right.

C The river on the left eventually becomes the Forth. Look out for grey wagtails, that is, any 'ordinary' or pied wagtail that shows creamy yellow below.

TROSSACHS WAGONWAYS

4 miles (6.5km)   Easy, except for short, steep section at start

The David Marshall Lodge is a Forestry Visitor Centre, gifted by the Carnegie Trust in 1960. It provides a network of trails, a large carpark and a refreshment stop for visitors. Perhaps slightly perversely, this walk starts from the car park, then goes away from the Lodge. However, it returns close to the

Lodge, where you might catch the café open. Thick screens of conifers hide the main road in places; the best views are at the start, but there is a fine waterfall right at the end of the walk. The route takes advantage of an old horse-drawn wagonway that ran from the slate quarries down to Aberfoyle. It is level after a steep but

short initial ascent. **Closely guard scampering children as you near the main quarry.** The path is interrupted by a number of small excavations into which the careless child might tumble. This is a good walk for a windy day, as the trees offer shelter at nearly all parts of the route.

6 *Bear right as the main quarry is reached and pick up the access road. Go down it, back towards the Duke's Road.*

7 *At the whitewashed cottage, go right and along the main road for a few minutes. Then go left (at time of writing) at a forestry track.*

1 *Leave your car in the **QEFP Visitor Centre** car park, above Aberfoyle on the Duke's Road. Walk back to the car park entrance and from the main road look for a path going uphill, above and opposite, right. Take care crossing the road.*

5 *The path, hitherto uneventful, needs* **GREAT CARE** *here. Unexpected 'mini-quarries' cut into the path. Three times you will be forced upwards into the dense conifers for a few yards and there are four diggings altogether. A very obvious reminder of how landscapes change: the slate workings are vanishing beneath a blanket of trees.*

4 *Enter forestry plantings via a rickety stile.*

3 *Turn right along a level path, the former wagonway, heading for the Highlands and noting the juniper.*

2 *Follow this path straight up the hill, ignoring a level track you shortly encounter on the way up.*

Map labels: Creag à Mhaclaidh · Lochan Reoidhte · Duke's Road · Hill Cottage · Quarry · Quarries · Allt a' Mhangan · Dismantled Tramway · A 821 · Quarry · Waterfall · Milton · Waterfalls · Queen Elizabeth Forest Park Visitor Centre · Aberfoyle · A 81 · A · B · C · D · E · P

Over

0   1 mile
0   1 km

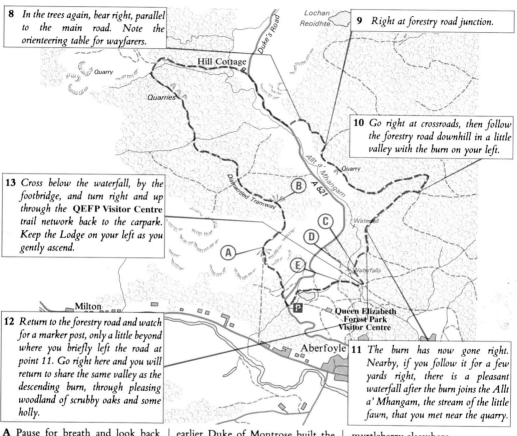

8 *In the trees again, bear right, parallel to the main road. Note the orienteering table for wayfarers.*

9 *Right at forestry road junction.*

10 *Go right at crossroads, then follow the forestry road downhill in a little valley with the burn on your left.*

13 *Cross below the waterfall, by the footbridge, and turn right and up through the **QEFP Visitor Centre** trail network back to the carpark. Keep the Lodge on your left as you gently ascend.*

12 *Return to the forestry road and watch for a marker post, only a little beyond where you briefly left the road at point 11. Go right here and you will return to share the same valley as the descending burn, through pleasing woodland of scrubby oaks and some holly.*

11 *The burn has now gone right. Nearby, if you follow it for a few yards right, there is a pleasant waterfall after the burn joins the Allt a' Mhangam, the stream of the little fawn, that you met near the quarry.*

Map labels: Lochan Reoidhte, Duke's Road, Hill Cottage, Quarry, Quarries, Allt a' Mhangam, Disused Tramway, A 821, Quarry, Waterfall, Waterfall, Waterfalls, Milton, Queen Elizabeth Forest Park Visitor Centre, Aberfoyle, B, C, D, A, E, P

A Pause for breath and look back towards the lowland edge. From here, the Macgregors would have watched the old drove road that lay further to the east, near the David Marshall Lodge, and planned their next raid on the lands of the Duke of Montrose. Flanders Moss is seen south-eastwards.

B A view northwards this time. An earlier Duke of Montrose built the road that now links Aberfoyle and the Trossachs, partly as a consequence of the numbers of visitors following the publication of Sir Walter Scott's *The Lady of the Lake*. Ben An is a little to the left of the whitewashed solitary cottage.

C Note the bilberry underfoot, often called blaeberry in Scotland and myrtleberry elsewhere.

D The waterfall of the Allt a' Mhangam.

E There are edifying notices at intervals, the most mind-boggling of which relates that each of us uses .85 tonnes of wood every year. It does much to explain the numbers of conifers seen on the walk.

BRIG O' TURK AND THE TROSSACHS VIEWPOINT

6 miles (9km)   Moderate

This route is best walked on a clear day, to appreciate the celebrated viewpoint, though the tree cover gives plenty of shelter. Brig o' Turk has nothing to do with exotic nationalities; the word 'tuirc' is Gaelic for wild boar. Sadly, they died out towards the end of the 16th century.

1 *If coming from Callander, park beyond the bridge at Brig o' Turk, that is, round the first bend on the left, just before a Forestry Commission sign for Achray Forest. Then walk back to the bridge and Brig o' Turk, turning right at a sign indicating a footpath to 'Duke's Pass, 1½'.*

2 *Follow track, which should be sign-posted Aberfoyle, over bridge. Ben Venue is on your right.*

13 *The path shortly starts downhill. Ben Venue is seen through the treetops on the left. There is also a glimpse of Loch Katrine from a ride a little below.*

12 *In the plantation, the path is almost hidden for a stretch by spruce branches sweeping low on one side, and larches on the other.*

11 *Cross the bridge and vanish thankfully into the woodlands on the right. Go up the left bank of the burn (looking upstream), on a faint, wet path. Very shortly cross the water and reach a broken gate. Go through gate and into thick plantation.*

10 *Turn your back on the indicator and walk south, along a faint path which drops through birch and bracken, to reach the main road near a carpark, at the bridge of the Easan Gruamach, the 'grumbling burn'.* **BE VERY CAREFUL** *- there is a steep bank to the roadside.*

9 *Up through the bog myrtle to cross the main road (TAKE CARE) and climb to the indicator.*

3 *Go through farmyard, over stile and turn left at junction in open country.*

4 *Enter plantings by main forestry road.*

5 *At road junction, go neither right nor left on the road, but instead straight ahead by a path, near the line of oaks. It should be waymarked with a yellow ring.*

6 *Cross a forestry road. The path is a little tricky to see, but it climbs slightly right. If in doubt, stay in the ride till you pick it up.*

7 *Go right, on to forestry road, which continues to climb gently.*

8 *At junction of three forest roads, look ahead for the path, running along the firebreak. The hilltop indicator will also become visible through the tree tops ahead.*

Map labels: The Trossachs; Pass of Trossachs; Trossachs Hotel; Achray Water; Loch Achray; Brig o' Turk; Brig o' Turk P; Loch Achray Hotel; Achray; Allt a' Choin reidhe; Ford P; Easan Gruamach; A821; Duke's Road; D; A; C; B

Over

18 Turn right, down narrower forestry track which is much more overgrown than the track passed previously.

19 Go right again, just before the track ends.

20 Cross the main road carefully and rejoin path going north-east diagonally down to Loch Achray.

21 Note picnic site and rejoin the Forest Drive, going east along the shore of the loch.

22 Leave the loch shore, go through a field and left at the junction, to return to the bridge and hence Brig o' Turk.

17 Continue down, with a road running parallel on the right. Ben An is conspicuous ahead. Pass one forestry access track on right.

16 Rejoin forestry road, turn right.

15 A pleasing clearing, followed by a footbridge to cross. Approach quietly and you may see black grouse, large dark birds with white on their wings.

14 Meet a main forestry road. Cross over, as the path continues.

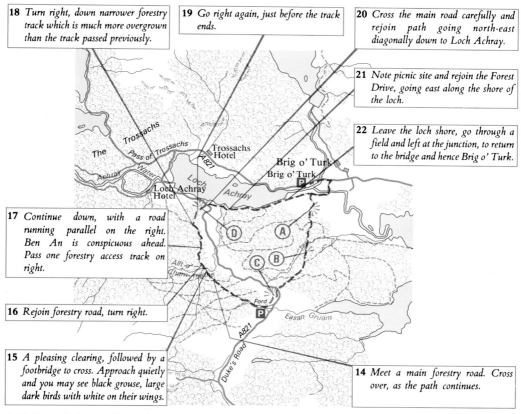

A Birds to look out for include siskins, pleasingly patterned in yellow/green and black. They have increased with the spread of coniferous plantations. Also look eastwards for an end-on view of Loch Venachar.

B Note view behind you into Glen Finglas.

C Viewpoint. The 19th-century minor poet Henry Chauncey Townshend in *A Descriptive Tour in Scotland*, published in 1840, climbed up from the Aberfoyle side with a companion. They found: 'Half the horizon was filled with mountains, tossed and tumbled about like an ocean arrested in its wildest rage.' The sight made them: 'Shout aloud with wonder and delight'. Here is the spot at which they shouted. As you have walked to this spot, you are also permitted at least a murmur of appreciation. The Trossachs lochs are there to identify with the help of the indicator and there is a wide choice of hills, though Ledi is not at its most impressive.

D A fine prospect of Loch Achray ahead, with birch and bog myrtle in the foreground.

Walk 17
BEN AN - A TROSSACHS VIEW
2 miles (3.5km) + 1200ft (360m) Strenuous

Ben An is, in mountain terms, not particularly high - a mere 1520 ft (454m). But it fits into the general scheme of the Trossachs very well - giving the impression of rugged, almost unapproachable, grandeur in spite of its small scale. It makes a pleasant afternoon's walk for the fit and well-shod, though the last section is steep. The route described here is of the there-and-back-again variety, but its view makes it amply rewarding. Over the last few years a path has become increasingly conspicuous leading off the summit crags north-west and turning down towards the shore of Loch Katrine; please disregard it, as the Strathclyde Water Board prefers that you return the way you came up. Besides, the forbidden path is slippery, vague and blocked by fallen trees. Climb Ben An on a clear day and the panorama, except to the north, is stunning.

6 *Take care as the path reaches the base of the cone, as it can be slippery. Note the little path going off left to the base of the rocks, for the benefit of rock climbers. Ignore it, as you take the main right fork and find yourself with a stiff upward pull.*

7 *You share your upward route with a stream.*

8 *Do not be tempted by a seeming shortcut on the left through a cleft, as the path begins mercifully to flatten out. Continue round to the col behind the main peak, as this is a safer route.*

9 *Retrace your steps, taking care on the steep descent.*

1 *The path starts opposite the car park a little west of the Trossachs Hotel, near the west end of Loch Achray. It is rocky and climbs relentlessly through larch plantations.*

5 *Out of the trees, a conspicuous knoll is seen on the left. Divert for a foretaste of the view further up, then rejoin the path. N.B. if any members of the party are uneasy about the short, steep section seen ahead and to the right of Ben An's cone; then they could happily wait at this point for the party's return.*

4 *The stream is now in the trees and can be heard on your left. Shortly afterwards there is a clearing with, at time of writing, a thoughtfully-provided wooden seat. The path continues at the far end of the clearing and shortly crosses the stream again.*

3 *Going up the rocky bank of the Allt Inneir burn (on your right) the path is a little hard to see, but it crosses the burn. Follow it as it goes right again, into the trees.*

2 *Take the steepest route, straight ahead!*

A Just before you are hemmed in on both sides by the trees, look back over Loch Achray. You can see the Duke's Road climbing towards the viewpoint featured in Walk 16.

B After you wind round to the summit, take care on the steep southern face that suddenly appears at your feet. The full length of Loch Katrine spreads westwards. To the south, the lowland hills are conspicuous: Dumgoyne on the edge of the Campsies, then the Fintry and Gargunnock hills. Beyond Loch Achray, below, and Loch Venachar, behind, Dumyat (Walk 10) in the Ochils is another conspicuous top in the east, with the Forth Valley misty in the far south-east. Ben Ledi, then, further west, Ben More, Stobinian and a range of Perthshire hills are conspicuous. In line with the northern shore of Katrine, but quite far to the north-west is the triangle of Ben Lui. To complete the view, more high peaks west of Loch Lomond can be seen, among them the distinctive craggy top of The Cobbler. Ben Lomond looms round the right edge of nearby Ben Venue.

THE LOCH KATRINE DAM

3 miles (5km)   Easy, with optional difficult 1 mile (1.5km)

Most of today's visitors are decidedly unfamiliar with the literary output of Sir Walter Scott. Hence the landmarks of *The Lady of the Lake*, his long narrative poem, are much less studiously sought out than they once were. The 'wild and strange retreat' of Ellen Douglas, in the third canto, is set in Coire nan Uruisgean, which today's maps still faithfully mark as the Goblins' Cave. It is conspicuous from the Strathclyde Water Board road that runs along Loch Katrine's north bank, or from Ben An (Walk 17), and is a gash and a rockfall on the slopes of Ben Venue.

It lies on the wildest part of Loch Katrine's shores, reached by the Bealach nam Bo - the pass of the cattle - a name with historical rather than literary overtones. The main drove road for cattle from the west lay along the south shore of Katrine. This short walk traverses part of it.

7 *As you go over the gate, you will see a stile, left. Go over it and follow path down by a rocky outcrop to the dam. Take care if children are present. Cross the dam.*

8 *Go right, past the dwelling house, on to the tarmac road.*

9 *Turn right at main road.*

6 *Return to the metal gate.*

10 *Look out for faint path going off right, to cut the corner. It starts just before the road goes sharply left.*

11 *Rejoin main road, turn right and return to the hotel entrance drive and car park.*

5 *(If continuing for a closer view of the bealach and Loch Katrine). Go through gate. The path now has a stream on the right (note the conspicuous holly tree on its bank), but shortly crosses it, continuing to keep to the lowest point in the temporarily narrowing valley. Divert right to knoll, a few yards away.*

4 *If short of time the second fence with its metal gate is your turning point. Continue from point 6.*

1 *Park in the Loch Achray Hotel car park, then walk round to the back of the hotel till you see a sign for 'Forest Walks', taking you gently upwards and right.*

2 *Take right fork at wide forestry road junction.*

3 *Go over a ladder-stile at a high fence. The path follows a fence on the right; keep to the pass straight ahead.*

A The Bealach nam Bo appears as a notch on the skyline ahead.

B View of the amphitheatre that opens out ahead of you. Ahead looms the pass, with its dramatic rock fall and solitary tree against the skyline. Below right is Loch Katrine with the Strathclyde Water Board road snaking along the opposite shore. In the summer season the steamship *Sir Walter Scott* may float into view to make the perfect picture. Do not be tempted by the path ahead. It goes as far as a gate on the far side of the enclosure, then the path deteriorates to make the pass no place for the leisurely walker.

C Loch Katrine holds 14,212 million gallons of water, largely the result of the average annual rainfall of 2,150mm (84.4 inches) on the loch itself. It supplies Glasgow's water.

Walk 19
BEN VENUE
6.5 miles (10.5km) + 2100ft (640m) Very difficult; attempt only in fine weather

Ben Venue, like many of the other hills hereabouts, is mentioned in Scott's *The Lady of the Lake*. The route of descent described here, for strong walkers only, outflanks the 'Crags, knolls and Mounds, confusedly hurl'd/The fragments of an earlier world' but needs the greatest of care. **Only fit, properly equipped walkers in good weather should attempt it. Take an additional map: OS 1:50 000, Sheet 57.** The chosen way up is by Gleann Riabhach, which is, frankly, tedious in its lower section through unrelieved conifers. However, this is a walk in which patience is rewarded. After the trees are left behind, there is the satisfaction of emerging on to the windy pastures of the upper glen, a remote spot quite unseen from any of the Trossachs roads. As you gain the crest of the pass, the westward views are stunning, all the way to the hill's twin tops. A word of caution is necessary: because of the longish walk-in, inexperienced walkers may not feel up to the direct descent to the Loch Katrine dam, which is practically pathless (in spite of some OS maps' indications to the contrary). Tired legs would be safer returning by the same route as the ascent. If you intend to make this a circular walk, confirm your decision from the summit, and then only if the weather looks clear. Without wishing to overstress the point, the direct descent to Loch Katrine is probably the most 'dangerous' section described anywhere in this book. Allow at least two and a half to three hours for reaching the summits and the same again for the descent, even though the Loch Katrine descent looks shorter.

A Ben Venue looks impressive through the trees, right.

B Within the first few minutes of your ascent up this steep rocky section, note how The Cobbler, with its distinct broken profile, appears round the right of the near hill behind you (Beinn Bhreac) while Ben Lomond's cone is almost in direct line. Loch Arklet is the next loch to appear, left of Loch Katrine. Ben Lui is also particularly conspicuous as a sharp cone above the right or north bank of Loch Katrine, though much further west. Note how the path seems to shelter from the prevailing winds by keeping just below the edge of the summit ridge.

C There are spectacular end-on views eastwards, of Loch Achray and, beyond, Loch Venachar, stretching back towards Callander. Loch Drunkie lies to the right of these. The white hotel buildings, your starting point, can also be seen.

D Look for Ben Ledi, left of Callander to the east. It shows a long ridge from this angle. Moving round anti-clockwise, Stuc a' Chroin and Ben Vorlich near Lochearnhead are in line. Ben Lawers above Killin is noticeable, as is the distinct hummocky profile of Meall nan Tarmachan, its less well-known neighbour to the west. Further round, you can see the big hills above Glen Dochart and beyond; look especially for Ben More and Stobinian, the largest on the skyline to the north-west, again in line, with Stobinian the nearer, showing the long ridges that drop down to Balquhidder, from an oddly foreshortened angle. Further west are more Munros, climbable from upper Balquhidder or Crianlarich. Then after Ben Lui, you come round to the Arrochar hills. After Ben Lomond, there are high hills to the south. Just a few points to the west of south, you should be able to see the profile of the Arran Hills. Then views of Glasgow buildings appear through the gap near Dumgoyne, the hump at the end of the Campsies to the south. Round beyond these lower moors, the end of the Pentlands behind Edinburgh might be visible and, if the smoke from the Grangemouth refinery is blowing away from the river, the Forth Bridges should be seen. Then it is round to the Ochils and back towards Ben Ledi.

Over

0 _____ 1 mile

0 _____ 1 km

14 *It must be repeated: if in any doubt about your own or your party's fitness, go back the way you came.*

13 *The old fence posts, as well as the path, will lead you to the second top.*

1 *The Loch Achray Hotel, your starting point, is at the west end of Loch Achray, with Ben Venue looming behind it. Park in the hotel car park. This is also the start of the Loch Katrine Dam Walk (18). Go round to the back of the hotel and turn right, which was signed 'Forest Walks' at time of writing.*

12 *As you reach the first cairned top, remember this is a high level path. You must 'look well to each step'. The other top with its triangulation point should be dead ahead, given clear conditions.*

11 *Follow path on and up. The broken fence posts guide you towards the top. Take your time here and enjoy the views.*

10 *A substantial cairn marks the junction of the Kinlochard path. The summit path goes right.*

9 *As the path steepens, marker posts are few; keep the main stream on your left and head slightly further west.*

8 *Beyond, on the open hill, the path is fainter, but head for the lowest point on the skyline ahead, a little to the right of the direction from which you emerged from the trees, and a little west of north. There are several wet patches.*

2 *At first fork, go left.*

3 *At first crossroads, go straight over.*

4 *Wide track stops, but the way up a narrower path is clear.*

5 *Rejoin a forestry road, turning left. Continue on the forestry road for a couple of minutes until a sign indicates the path right and uphill.*

6 *The track is quite clear all the way to the boundary fence, though showing signs of wear in places.*

7 *The forest edge fence had, at time of writing, a vertical stile surrounded by peat soup, the whole resembling an assault course and definitely not recommended for vertigo sufferers.*

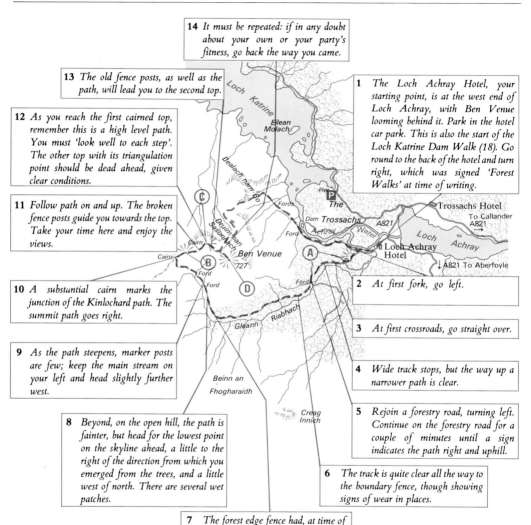

Over

0   1 mile
0   1 km

THE INSTRUCTIONS BELOW SHOULD BE FOLLOWED CLOSELY AND READ BEFORE STARTING THE DESCENT

18 *Beyond the lochan, you will see the dark rocks below of the Bealach nam Bo, the old droving route along Loch Katrine. The fence-posts swing right and down, but the way is pathless. Go right and stay near the posts, though always choosing the safest route.*

19 *When two tiny islets are in sight on Loch Katrine below, and you can see a little of the 'Sir Walter Scott' tied up at the Trossachs pier (unless, of course, it is out on the loch!) you may prefer to drop left into another gully with a burn, which descends parallel with the posts.*

17 *As the gully is trackless and has some boot-trapping holes, take care on a momentarily steep part, just before reaching an unexpected flat area, heather-covered, called the Druim nan Sasunnach, 'ridge of the lowlander'. The fence-posts swing left, westwards, away from your destination, but* **YOU MUST FOLLOW THEM,** *or risk entanglement in crags and rock below. Soon you reach a little lochan, which should have been noted earlier from above.*

20 *A gate at the meeting place of two other fences will come into view ahead. Aim for this gate, but the last and lowest part is as steep as anywhere encountered above, so continue to make a careful and controlled descent.*

21 *When you reach the gate, go right, through it. A faint path takes you back east. DO NOT go all the way to the Katrine shore, but keep a fence on your right.*

16 *Go through the line of fence-posts, but immediately turn a little right to follow them down, via a grassy and bilberry-filled gully. The posts should be on your right.*

22 *Follow this path (crossing several streams) back towards the Katrine dam, noting the crag on your right that made the westward diversion necessary.*

15 *If you intend to take the Loch Katrineside route down, return to the lowest point between the two summits and drop down to the right, immediately after the steep rock-face above on your right. You should see below a line of old fence-posts.*

24 *Follow this forestry road along the Achray Water, finding yourself eventually at the fork mentioned at point 2. Bearing left, retrace your steps to the car park.*

23 *Go through gate, keeping high fence on your left. (N.B. do not go over stile, left, but keep on path ahead.) A few hundred yards ahead there is a ladder stile. Go over this and on to the forestry road.*

Map labels: Loch Katrine, Eilean Molach, Bealach nam Bo, Druim nan Sasunnach, C, B, Cairn, Cairn, Ben Venue 727, Ford, Ford, Ford, D, Fords, Pier, The Trossachs, P, Dam, Ford, Achray, Water, A821, Loch Achray Hotel, Loch Achray, A821 To Callander, A821 To Aberfoyle, A, Gleann Riabhach, Beinn an

LOCH ARD AND ITS FOREST
3 miles (5km)   Easy

This walk is an undemanding couple of hours. The path first follows the south shore of Loch Ard, then goes up through plantations to a fine view of the loch before dropping to meet the track by which you came. A good walk for a windy day as the trees give shelter. There is an extension possible by following the waymarked lowest track westward to Kinlochard, returning by a loop, but the views are severely curtailed and the way made monotonous by endless conifers. The suggested route only goes as far as a viewpoint up the length of Loch Ard.

4 Rob Roy's Cave is on the right but hidden by trees now. Keep to the track.

3 At the fork, keep to the lower track, blue and red waymarked at time of writing. (You will return by the other track).

2 Go through the gate and past the cottage called Lochend, to reach the narrows of Loch Ard on their way to becoming the River Forth, a surprisingly domestic scene with boathouses and swans.

5 Very shortly after the waterside viewpoint, the return route runs uphill and back, on the left. Take this path.(The original path continues, however, and will take you on to Kinlochard. Energetic people may wish to walk further, but as noted above, the route is overshadowed by dense plantations.)

6 Be patient, the views will begin to open up as height is gained.

7 After dropping steeply downhill once more, turn right at junction and return to the car park.

1 On the B829 Aberfoyle-Stronachlachar road, there is well-disguised car park entrance at Milton, about a mile beyond Aberfoyle. Turn left across a bridge as soon as you see a postbox in the wall of an old mill building, then turn right and follow signs to Craigmuick Cottage, till you reach the Forestry Commission car park, your starting point. Walkers reach the loch by going back down the road from the car park, then turning left to follow red waymarkers.

A Ben Lomond dominates the western horizon in this view of Little Loch Ard. Note also Helen's Rock, a face dropping steeply into the loch on the opposite bank. This is also known as Echo Rock because of the remarkable acoustic properties hereabouts.

B Another peaceful spot by the water's edge, this time giving a full-length view of the loch. (Approach quietly in spring to hear the frogs' croak!) Note Ledard Glen on the far shore. Listen for the cackle of jays, too, a species of patchy distribution in Scotland, though benefiting from the kind of intensive forestry in which you are now standing.

C A series of westward views along the full length of the loch.

41

Walk 21
GLEN GYLE AND LOCH KATRINE
10 miles (16km)   Easy

Take advantage of the fact that the road round most of Loch Katrine is open only to Strathclyde Water Board vehicles. Walkers (and cyclists) have it more or less to themselves, making it easy for extra cautious or ill-shod pedestrians to escape a little from the motor car. Most visitors discover this for themselves at the Trossachs car park at the east end; fewer, though, start their excursions from Stronachlachar pier in the west. While the former is the domain of Sir Walter Scott, Glen Gyle is the territory of the real Rob Roy Macgregor. If you are prepared to take a whole morning or an afternoon for the excursion, then walk round beyond Portnellan to a sad little graveyard, protected from the deepened waters. Here many of the clan sleep, their fields now flooded through industrial man's lowland needs. You pass the birthplace of Rob Roy on the way; it is now a private house. Another Macgregor graveyard is nearby. The skyline in the west now has pylons striding along it, where once the cattle were brought down for the lowland sales. As the black beasts passed by his front door, so to speak, it is little wonder that the young Rob decided that cattle would be his trade. Take plenty of film and stroll as far as time permits, keeping an eye on upper Glen Gyle for any changes in the weather. As Loch Katrine is a water supply, camping, bathing, fishing, boating are all definitely forbidden and picnicking is not encouraged - but for scenery like this, with the comfort of a properly surfaced road, it is a very small price to pay.

A As you start, from Stronachlachar pier, note Factor's Island, just offshore where Grahame of Killearn, the Duke of Montrose.'s factor, was held to ransom by Rob and his band. The island would have been larger before the water level was raised.

B Looking right, Ben An can be seen at the far end of the loch.

C View of Portnellan on the opposite bank, the site of the first house occupied by Rob Roy after his marriage. A little to the right can be seen what look like railings on the shore: this is the old Clan Gregor graveyard.

D First view of Glengyle House (private).

E This quiet part of Katrine is the haunt of surprising numbers of wildfowl. Any species showing a lot of white at this range might be either goosander - very white, but the male has a red bill, or goldeneye - with a fast wing beat, making the bird appear to flicker black and white, and a white patch at the base of its bill.

F Opposite Glengyle House, ahead lies upper Glen Gyle, with the old drove road following the line of the disfiguring pylons. (They come in from the Ben Cruachan Hydro-Electric Power scheme.) The hill blocking the end is Ben Ducteach; beyond lies Loch Lomond. A little further to the right is a pass in from upper Balquhidder, the Bealach nan Corp, suggesting that funeral parties made their way into this glen. Upper Glen Gyle, according to tradition, was also the site of a lost village. Everywhere, now, the hills have only sheep, though a few cattle are also grazed in the glen. Try to imagine the scene with much broader fields in front of the house and the east-west traffic of drovers and pedlars bringing life to this now empty valley.

G In wet weather, from the bridge, note the conspicuous waterfall, the Sput Dubh, coming off the crags high above Glengyle House.

H The causeway leads to the second graveyard. When the loch, raised by the waterworks, threatened to cover the original site of the stones, they were moved to their present site. This is the place where Wordsworth was inspired to write *Rob Roy's Grave*. Sadly, he was wrong, as Rob himself is buried at Balquhidder, but William and Dorothy were lucky to see these stones in their original positions, at least 10ft (3m) below the strange embankment on which they now appear. Donald Glas of Glengyle (Rob's uncle) is, however, thought to lie here, though time has quite defaced the inscriptions.

Over

42

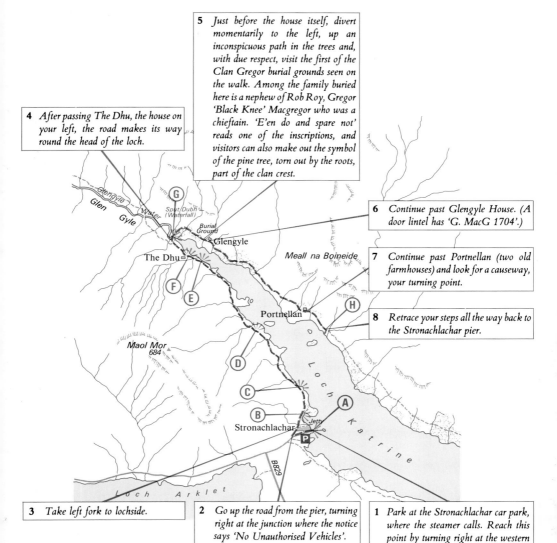

5 *Just before the house itself, divert momentarily to the left, up an inconspicuous path in the trees and, with due respect, visit the first of the Clan Gregor burial grounds seen on the walk. Among the family buried here is a nephew of Rob Roy, Gregor 'Black Knee' Macgregor who was a chieftain. 'E'en do and spare not' reads one of the inscriptions, and visitors can also make out the symbol of the pine tree, torn out by the roots, part of the clan crest.*

4 *After passing The Dhu, the house on your left, the road makes its way round the head of the loch.*

6 *Continue past Glengyle House. (A door lintel has 'G. MacG 1704'.)*

7 *Continue past Portnellan (two old farmhouses) and look for a causeway, your turning point.*

8 *Retrace your steps all the way back to the Stronachlachar pier.*

3 *Take left fork to lochside.*

2 *Go up the road from the pier, turning right at the junction where the notice says 'No Unauthorised Vehicles'.*

1 *Park at the Stronachlachar car park, where the steamer calls. Reach this point by turning right at the western junction of the B829.*

43

LOCH KATRINE AND THE START OF THE AQUEDUCT
4.5 miles (7.5km)   Easy, though moderate when not on roadways

This walk follows the line, above ground, of a tunnel bored through the ridge that separates Loch Katrine from Loch Chon. It carries Glasgow's water supply on the start of its 26 mile (42km) journey from Loch Katrine and was started in 1855. Royal Cottage, which the walk skirts, is the draw-off point and was so named from Queen Victoria's visit in 1859 to open the works officially. The first part is along a metalled road where only the occasional Strathclyde Water Board vehicle will interrupt a delightful vista. Once over the rough ground of the ridge, the return walk is by a public road, only justifiable for the fine views of Arklet. Nevertheless, this is one of the most scenic routes to walk anywhere in the Trossachs. The solitude of the high ground is in contrast to the scene in the 1850s, when the area swarmed with gangs of navvies. Please note that the shafts mentioned along the length of tunnel are more strictly towers and it is quite impossible to see into them, let alone fall down them.

A The supply from Loch Arklet over the hill, right, drops down to the main reservoir, via a series of quite impressive, though entirely artificial, cascades dating from 1895. Looking the other way, Factor's Island lies just off the Stronachlachar pier, while in the east Ben An's distinctive hump marks the heart of the Trossachs.

B An open, ever-changing view of hill and loch. Cameras at the ready.

C Just before leaving the surfaced road, look back, west, across the loch where both Portnellan and Glengyle House can be seen. Each has associations with the Macgregors (see Walk 21).

D As you cross, look for the conspicuous shaft of the outgoing aqueduct. This looks like a circular, blank, stone-built tower. Beneath your feet are two tunnels, each of about 1½ miles (2.4km) length, taking water gently towards Frenich at the end of Loch Chon (Walk 23 traces the next section of aqueduct). Look up to the skyline, where a slightly surreal collection of other tower-like structures marks the course of this Victorian engineering feat.

E To reach this optional viewpoint, leave the path momentarily at an inconspicuous fork. The main path skirts the topmost knoll to the right, but on top, near another obelisk, there is a fine view towards the Balquhidder peaks, northwards, and an unexpected view of Ben Lomond to the south. Lock Arklet lies to the west.

F A splendid end-on view of Loch Arklet. This view must be one of the most constantly-changing in all the Highlands. Loch Lomond, lying out of sight beyond the end of Arklet, can often be in squalls, while the nearer loch is flooded with sunlight. Keep film for this one. Arklet itself was increased to three times its size in order to supplement supplies from Loch Katrine. While looking down this lonely glen, consider that in Rob Roy's day, there was a township of around twenty houses at Corrie-arklet, the settlement on the right hand or northern bank.

Over

1 *If driving, go right at the western junction of the B829 and park at the Stronachlachar car park, where the steamer calls. Go back up the drive, turn left, then second left to gain the road that runs along the south bank of Loch Katrine. The sign says 'Reservoir Area, No Unauthorised Vehicles'.*

2 *Continue along this picturesque surfaced road. It carries only Strathclyde Water Board traffic and follows the old drove road down Glen Gyle (at the far west end of Katrine) and over the Bealach nam Bo (see Walk 18). Note, left, the hill passes on the far shore which the Macgregors would have used to travel to upper Balquhidder.*

3 *Just before the cattle grid, fence and wall, turn right, joining a track that goes up with the stream on your left.*

4 *Cross over little footbridge.*

13 *Take the third turning on the right to return to the pier.*

5 *Go over fence; the path is conspicuous enough.*

6 *After a short wettish section, go past a strange obelisk, devoid of any markings, presumably an aid to surveying the line of the tunnel. The path kinks uphill here.*

12 *Turn right at the road junction.*

7 *If dropping off the knoll, take care that you do not do so too literally, as the heather is steep and slippery.*

8 *Go over ladder-stile and into coniferous plantation.*

11 *Turn right and be patient on this road section, the first part is less interesting and a little hemmed-in by conifers.*

10 *Follow this path back to the road, enjoying the stream which flows on the left.*

9 *At first shaft in the forest, take care to follow the path going left and into the woodland. This avoids the slippery slope beyond the shaft.*

Stronachlachar

Jetty
Eilean Dharag
(Factor's Island)

L o c h   K a t r i n e

Aqueduct Outlet

Aqueduct Intake

Loch Arklet

B 829

Pier
Boat House
Cattle Grid
271
Meall Meadhonach
Royal Cottage
Shaft
278
Tom Ard
Shaft
Faery Knoll
Shaft

Stuc Gille Chohnuill . 392

Lochan Mhàim nan Carn

Loch Chon

0   1 mile
0   1 km

Walk 23
AROUND LOCH CHON
6 miles (10km)   Easy

This is a walk which shows that the visitor need not stray too far from the public road to be rewarded with some solitude. Its gradients are negligible and the unexpected presence of an aqueduct keeps the interest up on the west bank where mature trees obscure some of the views. Loch Chon is said to be haunted by a dog-headed monster that swallows passers-by. This warning should ensure children are well-behaved on its banks. Other wildlife interest includes jays, buzzards and herons. This walk is one of a number of Forestry Commission routes within the Queen Elizabeth Forest Park, but it also approaches farmland at the loch's north end and **dogs should be very firmly on a lead.**

13 *Go through gap in wall, immediately after man made cave, giving aqueduct access - there is another obvious section of aqueduct nearby. Then cross stream close to another visible section.*

12 *On left, an identical shaft to that mentioned at F. Go straight on. This marks an approximate halfway point, about one and a half hours after leaving the carpark. The next section is through a pleasant, comparatively open ride.*

11 *Cross bridge and bear right.*

10 *Path plunges back into mature conifers, with a scattering of ancient oaks, and crosses two footbridges.*

9 *The next section has open views over loch and a gently rising and falling gradient.*

8 *Note path merging on right. Carry on to loch side.*

7 *On passing the last of the buildings on your right, look out on the same side for a forest road.*

1 *Take the cul-de-sac road to Inversnaid from Aberfoyle. About 7 miles (11km) along it and after little Loch Dhu is the Loch Chon Car Park, signposted by the Forestry Commission. This is your starting point.*

2 *Walk back to the public road and turn right. When a sign to a boat launching place is seen, turn right down to the loch shore.*

3 *Turn left along a faint path, sometimes boggy underfoot. Cross a stream, following the bank of a twisty river connecting Lochs Chon and Dhu.*

4 *Beyond the tree, the path splits. Take the drier one, heading back towards the road.*

5 *At the road turn right.*

6 *Turn right at the Loch Dhu House road and go over bridge. Follow road to houses.*

B829

Shaft.
Shaft
Quarry (disused)
Foot Bridge
French Farm
G
Loch Chon
Shaft
F
H
Heron Island
E
D
Shafts
Aqueduct
C
P
Boathouse
A
Loch Dhu
Loch Dhu House
B

Over

46

15 *This pleasant stretch of path continues through bracken till it reaches a track, which leads you to the main road. Note the view back to Ben Lomond from the track.*

16 *Rejoin public road which runs downhill and gives a view of Loch Chon. Turn right.*

17 *If time is short, it is quicker to keep to the road back to the car park. It is more interesting, however, to divert where possible, along the bank. The first of these opportunities comes with a bracken-covered wall. Follow it down to the shore to pick up faint path, passing picnic sites, then return to road, noting shortly after, an old milepost (Aberfoyle 8 miles, Stronachlachar 3¼). Make sure you are walking towards Aberfoyle!*

14 *Third shaft and large stream come into view. Cross by the footbridge. Go through a small brown gate. DO NOT TURN RIGHT on to Frenich Farm property. Continue through 'kissing gate' - only a few paces further - and shortly reach an open ride.*

18 *Option to leave the road, following the bank closely, crossing stream and climbing fence almost immediately.*

19 *Only the faintest of paths hereabouts.*

21 *Opposite the next island, the shore path becomes clearer, indicating your nearness to the car park and your starting point. Continue along it till it reaches the far end of the car park itself.*

20 *After walking round promontory, climb fence and find route along steep bank, reminding yourself it is only fifty yards up to the public road should the thick bracken exasperate.*

A A splendid viewpoint by a magnificent oak where the river broadens into Loch Dhu. Note bridge at far end, which you will shortly cross.

B The pleasantly-scented wiry plant growing in the wet patches is bog myrtle. (Try it with pork chops.)

C At loch side, note Frenich Farm, your turning point at far end of loch.

D Wood sorrel, with clover-like leaves, grows below the larches after first footbridge.

E Overgrown spoil heaps on left indicate old tunnelling operations when aqueduct was built. Near the second footbridge a black iron-plated structure is a visible section of aqueduct. This carries water from Loch Katrine to Glasgow. On this shore, there are actually two separate aqueducts, of which the earlier, built in 1855, will become intermittently visible as the walk progresses. Beyond it, note common tormentil with its four small yellow petals and also the first of many short stone posts, indicating the position of the subterranean water channel.

F On left, note stone building, like a strange observatory with an iron lattice dome. This is an inspection shaft.

G Pause to admire open view northwards, with line of aqueduct disappearing towards Loch Katrine, over the hill range (Walk 22).

H Look out to Heron Island, a very logical place to expect to find these solitary fishers, though they are wary of disturbance.

47

Walk 24
LOCH LOMOND WOODS
8.5 miles (13.5km)   Some easy, some moderate, a few difficult places

The rugged nature of the Highland landscape often prevents the link-up of a satisfying circular route, but north of Rowardennan there is the unusual opportunity of taking in two versions of the West Highland Way. The high road is a forestry access road and, like all the others frequently encountered on the walks in this book, is easy both in gradient and underfoot. However, the low road is another matter. It twists through the oakwoods, presenting widely differing grades of walking from deluxe smoothed gravel to rocky shelves which the management powers have seen fit to supply with chained handrails for the timid. The whole route as described leaves the public road at Rowardennan and, after three-quarters of an hour's walking, gives you the choice of which half of the loop you wish to do first. The easier high track offers good viewpoints across to the high hills around Arrochar, while the low path offers adventure and, perhaps, even an encounter with (shy) wild goats! The walk as described goes out by the easy road, back by the more strenuous route. The turning point is an optional half-hour extension to the Rowchoish bothy, a shelter intended for the long-distance brigade, midway between Rowardenn and and Inversnaid. This is quite a big day out; make sure you are fully provisioned and equipped.

A If you can ignore the traffic noise from the opposite bank, even before you reac Ptarmigan Lodge, the woodlands typify the sentiment of the famous song about the 'bonnie banks'. The prolific bird population seems to think so too and a spring walk here is very rewarding. Garden warblers seem particularly common and can be recognised through being utterly devoid of any markings whatsoever - just a general dingy grey-brown. Their song, however, more than makes up for their less-than-exotic appearance.

B Notice the rhododendrons in this section, so beloved of west-coast landowners for privacy purposes. An alien species, rhododendrons are common all over the west of Scotland. As you walk along, consider how resistant they are to any efforts to get rid of them. Their glossy leaves resist chemical spraying, their wood is not easily burnt, and if cut down, they spring from the base. They destroy all ground cover and provide little or no food for birds. Even their nectar is poisonous and domestic animals will not graze them.

C The Cobbler to the north-west shows its spectacular silhouette near the ruined sheilings. Notice how the track has temporarily climbed up out of the oak woodlands that flank the loch into the spruce plantations higher up the hillside - some aspects of the view will be lost as the conifers grow.

D A momentary diversion to the left offers a fine view down the loch.

E ...and even better mountain views north-westward if you peer between the birches. Ben Narnain is flat-topped, next to The Cobbler, with Ben Vorlich further north.

F Go down to the shore for a low-level viewpoint at Rowchoish bothy. Good views northwards. Inversnaid, with public road access, is on the east bank. In hazy conditions, you can just make out the coaches that have made it down the hill. Across the water is Tarbet with the West Highland railway-line coming over from Loch Long on its way to Oban or Fort William and Mallaig. The Cobbler is still prominent on the skyline. The scenery is splendid - but the summer season traffic noise echoes across the waters on a still day.

G All around you and stretching away north are the lands of Craigroystan, once owned by Rob Roy Macgregor, at the height of his 'legitimate' career. As you make your way through the oaks it is hard to imagine that, according to 18th-century documents, one hundred and fifty families had their homes in the little townships scattered between Rowardennan and the head of the loch. Land once tilled has now returned to a kind of wilderness.

H Do not be surprised if you come across wild goats hereabouts; their ancestors have been here for generations. *Over*

7 *After retracing your steps from Rowchoish, stay on the bank this time, following the West Highland Way signs.*

6 *If intending to walk the Rowchoish detour, go right where the track peters out on the shore. You are on the West Highland Way. (Otherwise, go left, following on from point 7.)*

5 *At the fork go left to Rowchoish and the lochside.*

4 *Shortly after the first of the Arrochar Hills appears ahead on the far bank of Loch Lomond, on the left of the track you will see the start of the low-level section. Make your choice here. The route suggested continues on the higher track.*

Tarbet
—Pier

Rowchoish

Creag à
492
Bhocain

Rob Roy's
Prison

Ben Lomond
974

8 *The path climbs above the rocky drop known as Rob Roy's prison, where, it is said, he held his opponents confined, or even that he lowered them over the slabs into the water. Many stories attached themselves to him; sufficient to say that it is an odd spot, particularly on a still day, when it seems hard to work out exactly how far away the water is - take care not to lean out too far!*

731.
Ptarmigan

3 *Go right and uphill at the fork and through a gate.*

Ptarmigan
Lodge

2 *Make sure you continue right at the Youth Hostel fork, then left at the next fork, noting a West Highland Way marker.*

9 *Grey wagtails, tree creepers, sandpipers, bluebells, creeping jenny - all small distractions on a path that varies from well-gravelled to slippery and rocky. Please try to keep to a single track; lazy walkers searching for slightly easier ground on either side of a minor obstacle are the ones responsible for spreading of the main path.*

Rowardennan
Lodge

Rowardennan

Pier

Jetties
Caravan
site

Rowardennan
Hotel

Caravan
site

Inverbeg

10 *In many places, falling in to the loch would take more than a reasonable amount of silliness, but at this point it is enough of a possibility to justify the chained hand rail.*

11 *The path clearly climbs left and back up to the forestry road. At the road, turn right and retrace your steps.*

1 *The walk starts from the well-used Rowardennan car park, the terminus of the public road. Go northwards along the track from the car park.*

49

Walk 25

ROWARDENNAN WATERFALL

2 miles (3.5km)   Moderate

Walks from Rowardennan, by the nature of the landscape, are of two kinds; either quite long, as in Ben Lomond, or the Loch Lomond Woods walk (Walk 24) or quite short, as in this hour-and-a-half's worth of scrambling about in the woodlands. The walk is of interest for the difference between the two sorts of path that it uses. The first is - or was at time of writing - a little overgrown, but well-constructed, climbing steadily by the banks of the Ardess Burn through delightful wooded scenery with pleasing waterfalls. The second path, used on the way downhill, is the walkers' 'motorway' to and from Ben Lomond and, with its erosion problems, makes an interesting contrast. (The route to the top of 'The Ben' is first recorded in Ordnance Survey maps of the 1860s and '70s. Like other hills further east in the Trossachs, it had the proper credentials to attract the tourist, even in Victorian times. It was fairly accessible, a conspicuous objective and the highest point in the vicinity.) Take care on the way down if it is wet.

---

3 *Though there has been a stream below you, right, the path crosses another.*

4 *The oaks are left behind as you enter a thick plantation with scrubby birch growing closely round the path.*

5 *Continue to push steadily upwards, enjoying the scent of the bog myrtle crushed underfoot and intermittent glimpses of the slopes of Ben Lomond - as well as the tumbling Ardess Burn.*

2 *Before you reach the first fork (the left-hand track of which goes to the Youth Hostel) take a faint path going uphill on your right, into the oaks. It may be waymarked.*

6 *Path leaves the noise of the waters behind and swings momentarily right into thick conifers in an unexpectedly southerly direction before emerging on the main Ben Lomond path. Be prepared to stoop low under some of the encroaching conifers.*

1 *The large car park at Rowardennan is the starting point. Go northwards along the shore road that leads towards the Youth Hostel.*

8 *The path swings you right and away from the firebreak; follow the path down to the car park.*

7 *Go left and downwards. Glen Douglas is conspicuous straight ahead on the other side of the loch.*

A Shortly after, there is a good view from a firebreak back over to Loch Lomond as well as to the Sput Ban, the white waterfall, conspicuous in wet weather on the flanks of Ben Lomond above.

B There is a short digression possible here to another waterfall. Look for a point where the path broadens and climbs gently away right. The waterfall is reached by a faint path off left. Return to main path after viewing it.

C Another fine view over your shoulder down to the loch and the Youth Hostel, now surprisingly far below you.

D Road improvements, continuing high ownership of private vehicles, forestry interests channelling walkers in certain areas, and guidebooks, too, have all contributed to the obvious heavy usage to be noted on the main Lomond path; yet a recent report by The Countryside Commission for Scotland considers this path to have been in worse condition forty years ago. Note how the walkers are now, at least, kept in one line, rather than allowed to follow a wide number of 'braided' pathways.

SALLOCHY WOOD AND
THE BANKS OF LOCH LOMOND   2.5 miles (4km)   Easy

0   1 mile

0   1 km

Sample the famous banks of Loch Lomond without committing too much energy and time to the excursion. Walkers seeking more exercise in more rugged scenery should look at Walk 24, beyond Rowardennan. First-time visitors along this section of the Balmaha-Rowardennan road will find the celebrated shoreline an interesting combination of private property and public recreation areas, which has caused some headaches for the planners of the West Highland Way. This little walk takes advantage of part of a forestry trail, then joins the West Highland way for the return. It is an excursion on which even the habitual stern warning about footwear might just be suspended! Take care, though, on slippery tree-roots in the plantation and also near the viewpoint on the banks of Loch Lomond. Enjoy the birdsong of the oakwoods - from May onwards, dedicated birdwatchers will be sorting out the songs of wood warbler, garden warbler, redstart and tree-pipit, while the rest of the party will be enjoying the views across to Inchlonaig - the island of the yew trees, which were said to have been planted by Robert the Bruce to supply the Scottish bowmen.

2 Park and follow the path away from the loch and across the road, noting the change of woodland into managed plantation - which at time of writing has helpful little nameplates on some of the trees.

3 The path continues into the trees. Watch for slippery roots.

4 You pass the ruined hamlet of Wester Sallochy, swamped by gloomy conifers. Follow the path left, twisting past the old walls, then go right and up.

5 You emerge on to a forestry road. If you continue on the path, it takes you left to higher viewpoints beyond an old quarry, seen on the left. Instead, GO RIGHT on the forestry track.

1 On the continuation of the B837 4 miles (6.4km) north of Balmaha, look for the road signs to the Sallochy Wood car park, your starting point.

6 Cross the main road and on the shore side, look for a track heading down to the water's edge.

10 Enjoy this well-maintained final section back to the car park.

9 Follow the leftmost of two paths back to the shore.

8 To avoid a rocky outcrop, the path kinks right and up.

7 The path very soon joins the West Highland Way. Go right.

Sallochy Wood   Quarry   Rowardennan

Forest

Wester Sallochy

Loch

Lomond

Sallochy

A Strathcashel Point is in view as you stroll gently down the track.

B Very pleasing, open woodland with honeysuckle underfoot.

C A splendid viewpoint south to Inchlonaig and the other islands beyond. Luss is the village on the far bank. In summer, note the dense oak canopy immediately below. On the shore, peeping sandpipers are common in spring before too many visitors arrive.

CONIC HILL

3 miles (5km) + 1130ft (345m)   Mostly difficult; no dogs allowed

Conic Hill rises behind Balmaha on Loch Lomond. Though higher, it seems to match the shape of the islands that rise in a line from it out into the loch. Geologically, this is unsurprising as Conic Hill and the islands lie on the Highland Boundary Fault. Stand on its summit and you can truly look on two different landscapes and cultures. This walk takes advantage of part of the West Highland Way, but escapes it, as it becomes boggy, to ascend a little way for a switchback walk back along the rather confusing line of tops. The conglomerate rock of which the hill is constructed is a great geological pudding-mix. A red sandstone matrix holds together stained and water-rounded pebbles of various sizes, commonly of quartz and associated with the fault line. It can be a little treacherous to walk over; take care while descending the slope on the last of the hill's convex humps. There are continuous views all the way from the top of the pass (called a 'bealach' in Gaelic) and the walk is naturally most rewarding in clear weather. When driving towards the hill on the B837, pause at a convenient layby a mile or so short of Balmaha to study the profile of the hill, seen on the right. Your path goes along the skyline.

A Self-heal is the small purplish flower with a dense head. St John's Wort is taller, about 12 inches (30cms), with several yellow starry flowerheads. They grow along the track in high summer.

B Listen for thin high mewing - buzzards calling! They are common on the moorland around the hill.

C The distinct texture of the conglomerate rock is already apparent on the hill shoulder ahead. Note Stockie Muir in the distance, right, with the rocky line of the approach to The Whangie (Walk 32). The nearer dome of Duncryne Hill (Walk 30) at the south end of Loch Lomond is conspicuous behind the marshes of the Endrick mouth.

D As the path flattens out, there are the first views over long moorland slopes towards Ben Lomond, left, with the Arrochar Hills beyond, on the other side of the loch. Almost immediately, look for a short pathway joining from the heights above right. This is where you will rejoin later.

E From this top there are two tops visible looking back south-west, as well as a wide prospect of Loch Lomond itself. Look beyond the islands in line; in clear conditions the hills of Arran are visible beyond the Clyde, a distance of more than 40 miles (65km). In the opposite direction, try to pick out the Wallace Monument, on its crag beside Stirling. Southwards, the tower-blocks of Glasgow can also be seen, between the Kilpatricks and the Campsies. There are Highlands to the right and lowlands to the left - a very obvious contrast in landscapes.

F A last view of the islands without tops intruding. Inchcailloch is nearest, with Clairinsh just to the left, then, going out, Torrinch, Creinch and Inchmurrin. Notice how Ben Bowie on the far bank also lines up, marking the fault line. But it was the much more recent Ice Age, only ending 10,000 years ago, that carved out the loch in front of you, scouring a deep (600 feet; 183m) trench in the schists to the north, then broadening out where it met the lowland sandstones to form a shallower lowland loch of only around 75 feet (23m) depth. The dumped material from the glacier has kept the sea out, but Loch Lomond is only 27ft (8m) above sea level. Just as the Inveruglas Water (Loch Sloy, Walk 34) once drained eastwards, so the rivers in Glen Douglas and Glen Luss (up the loch on the far bank) once drained eastwards into the valley now occupied by the Endrick, until the Loch Lomond glacier cut through their courses. Now the Endrick flows west.

Over

0   1 mile

0   1 km

7 *Keep to the waymarked path while it continues to ascend gently, with the bulk of the hill blocking all views on the right. Note that there are other paths or sheep tracks disappearing up to the right.*

8 *AT THE HIGHEST POINT of the West Highland Way proper (where underfoot in wet weather it resembles peat broth) leave it for a short path that goes up and right on to a little pass between two areas of higher ground. Here there is another path. Go left.*

9 *You should now have reached the most easterly high top of Conic Hill. There is a small cairn.*

6 *Make your way round to the top of the 'bealach' or pass.*

5 *The path, which started level, bends upwards and left by way of some deluxe steps. Cross the stream at the top of the slope.*

4 *Go through kissing gate, noting lambing notices and warnings to keep to the path.*

3 *Take the second on the left and where track ends take the continuing path through mature conifers. Note the old Scots pine mixed with the tall larches.*

2 *Follow West Highland Way arrows (and a blue forest walk sign).*

10 *There is a faint and intermittent summit path. Follow it westwards along the line of the tops. (They can be a little confusing - there usually seems to be one more than you expect!) Note as you set off that the next top but one seems about the same height as your departure point. There are, however, four of roughly the same height.*

11 *Take great care on this lower top, where the path is lost among the knobbly rock. You will see the West Highland Way just below you.*

12 *You join the main path by going off right, at the top of the bealach. At time of writing there is a prominent pole. This is the path noted at point C on your way up.*

1 *There is a large car park in Balmaha, on the right going north. The walk starts from behind it. Go on to a forestry track and turn right.*

13 *Retrace your steps to the car park.*

F

Conic Hill
361

D

E

Bealach Ard

C

B

A

P

Balmaha Plantation

Loch

Jetties

Balmaha

B837

Pier

Auchingyle

Lomond

Inchcailloch

The Kitchen
(Crannog)

Walk 28

INCHCAILLOCH
2.5 miles (4km)   Mostly easy

This walk is a little different from the others: it is on an island. Inchcailloch can be reached by using the services of MacFarlane and Son, The Boatyard, Balmaha, Loch Lomond, G63 0JG, Tel: (01360) 870214. They run an on-demand ferry service to Inchcailloch, in addition to cruises on the loch, which also call at

Inchcailloch by arrangement. Phone them with the numbers in your party and arrange a suitable time. You can trot round the island in just over an hour (it is bigger than it first appears) but it is suggested you spend, at the very least, two hours, to soak up the atmosphere, enjoy the superb summit views, picnic, take pictures etc.

Inchcailloch is owned by the Nature Conservancy Council and the greatest respect must be paid to its woodlands: keep to the paths, keep your dog under the strictest control, and read the notice on landing. There is an excellent nature trail booklet available.

6 *Veer right and uphill to a diversion left to the 13th-century church, evidence of the vanished community. From here it is only a few minutes walk down left, then left again, back to the shore and the landing stage on the right.*

1 *Park in the main Balmaha car park, on the right going north. Go back and cross the main road.*

Opposite is a road down to the loch. Go down the road, turning right for the pier and the departure point.

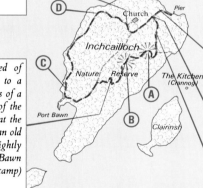

Loch Lomond

Pier

Jetties   Balmaha   B837

Church   Pier

Inchcailloch

Nature   Reserve   The Kitchen (Crannog)

Port Bawn   Clairinsh

2 *Disembark at North Bay. If the loch is high, there is a path going right, a few yards up the slope, otherwise walk along the shore to pick up the main path running into the wooded island.*

5 *The path, mainly constructed of railway sleepers, leads down to a junction. (There is the remains of a corn-drying kiln on the right of the path just before the junction, at the foot of the slope; it looks like an old drain.) Go left to the slightly unexpected camp-site at Port Bawn (written permission needed to camp) then back along the shore.*

3 *Turn left and cross a stream by a footbridge.*

4 *The oaks are replaced by alder trees where it is wet. Note how these alders have several trunks, suggesting they have been coppiced some time ago. Keep on the main path.*

A On your way to this viewpoint, there is a face of the lumpy conglomerate sandstone (familiar if you have already walked on Conic Hill). Higher up you look south to the island of Clairinsh (with its 'crannog', a 2000-year-old, man-made island at its left-most tip) and beyond to the Endrick marshes. Behind these are the Fintry Hills then (right), the Campsies and the Kilpatricks.

B But an even better view is to follow, looking north to the Highlands from the 250ft (75m) high summit: a huge panorama of island and mountain.

C Like Conic Hill, Inchcailloch has a band of serpentine running parallel to and north of the fault line. This metamorphic rock, seen in an outcrop just left of the path, looks dingy and is smoother than the conglomerate.

D The site of Inchcailloch Farm. Although the entire island, thickly wooded, looks natural, the oaks are mature trees that have grown up from the managed woodland which was a source of oak bark, used in the tanning industry. This stage in the history of Inchcailloch was from about 1770 till the end of the 19th century. Before that, the island was farmed; the Nature Conservancy Council's nature trail booklet gives further information.

GARTOCHARN AND
THE BANKS OF LOCH LOMOND 3.5 miles (5.5km) Easy

```
0                          1 mile
0            1 km
```

One of the easiest walks in this book, Gartocharn, bypassed by most of the tourist hurly-burly, sits contentedly in a patchwork of little fields, An important feature of the walk is its little foray into Shore Wood, part of the Loch Lomond National Nature Reserve. This reserve, in the care of the Nature Conservancy Council, consists of five islands - Creinch, Torrinch, Clairinsh, Aber Isle and Inchcailloch, all clearly seen from the shore - and a substantial part of the marshes around the mouth of the Endrick Water. Please note, only a part of Shore Wood is open without permission and it is important to keep strictly to the shore path. **Do not take dogs into the reserve and keep them on a lead while crossing fields.**

10 *A suggested turning point is in the vicinity of a second stile. Retrace your steps all the way back to the post-box at the junction at point 6.*

9 *Enter reserve at left-hand gate (carefully closing it behind you). Keep to the path, crossing a stile.*

8 *At next junction take left fork and follow the track down to the bank of the loch. After admiring the view from the water's edge, return to the track, going left to gate of reserve.*

11 *At post box turn right and follow road on.*

7 *At first junction, go straight on. At time of writing this was signed for the nature reserve.*

12 *Turn left at main road, left again by the toilets and so return to your starting point.*

6 *Look for a small post-box only about 100 yards (91m) further on. Turn right down track signed as a private road to a number of lochside houses.*

5 *The path goes down a short track, over second little bridge and through a gate on to a surfaced road. Turn right, then left at end of road.*

1 *Gartocharn is on the A811 south of Loch Lomond. Park sensibly in the village; there is some parking near the church, reached by turning left (if coming from Balloch) at the public toilets and following the road round to the right past the Police Station. The community centre is beyond the church to the east. Park, then go past the community centre and turn immediately left down the track beside the centre. Go through a kissing gate.*

4 *Do not cross fence; continue to follow field boundary till you reach a gate and a little railway-sleeper bridge on your left.*

3 *Track goes right and through kissing gate. Stream appears left.*

2 *Follow faint track down through field, keeping boundary hedge on your right.*

A Immediately a view of Loch Lomond opens up. Note the craft moored at Balmaha on the right-hand side of the loch and Ben Lomond dominating beyond.

B Given clear weather, this south bank offers fine views up the loch. Inchcailloch lies next to Balmaha with Clairinsh in front of it, though

Aber Isle is the nearest small islet. Moving west, Torrinch and Creinch line up along the Highland Boundary Fault, with a confusion of islands beyond.

C This reserve is important as it represents what was once a much more extensive habitat in Scotland. Most marshes like the one lying

further east as well as the oak-dominant woodland have now been lost in the lowlands, because of the needs of agriculture.

D After crossing stile, visitors in May will enjoy a sheet of bluebells, flowering before the dense oak canopy begins to cut down the sunlight.

DUNCRYNE HILL
2 miles (3.5km) maximum   Easy

```
0                                                          1 mile
0                                        1 km
```

Duncryne Hill itself is probably the shortest walk in the book, which is quite unfair, as it also has one of the best views! Combine this walk with one to the shores of Loch Lomond (Walk 29). On arrival at the edge of the wood that surrounds the western part of this extinct volcano, there is a neatly-lettered notice which reads: 'Duncryne is private. Well-behaved visitors are welcome to use the track and hill-top. Please do not wander into the woods (reserved for teddy-bears etc.) Help us by clearing litter, left by less tidy visitors. We hope you enjoy sharing our point of view.' No finer summary of the Country Code can be found. Duncryne Hill is first cousin to Dumbarton Rock, Dumgoyne and a number of other volcanic vents, that is, the inner core of a volcano, a whole series of which were responsible for the ancient Clyde Plateau lavas from which the Kilpatricks and Campsies (seen prominently from the top) are formed. Duncryne itself pokes through the Old Red Sandstone; fertile fields surround it, in spite of its position on the Highland edge. Its little dome is unmistakable, from whichever compass point you approach Gartocharn.

1 *Gartocharn is on the A811 south of Loch Lomond. Park sensibly in the village; there is some parking near the church, reached by turning left (if coming from Balloch) at the public toilets and following the road round to the right. This is the same parking place as used for Gartocharn and Loch Lomond (Walk 29). Go back to the main road, turn left, cross over and take first right, before the speed limit signs, just past the Gartocharn Hotel. Go up this quiet country road for about half a mile and look for a layby, left, at the very end of the woodland also on the left. Alternatively, if time is short, drive here and make this your starting point.*

4 *Retrace your steps to the village, noting that the reverse of the same notice at the layby on the return says 'Ladies and Gentlemen, if you have been, we thank you'!*

3 *A path leads right from the kissing gate, then left and straight to the top.*

2 *Teddy-bears or not, a stile gives access to the wood edge with its splendid notice, and another leads to an open field. Go straight across to the kissing gate.*

Police Sta.

Gartocharn

A811

A 142 Duncryne

A The view is quite unexpected and out of all proportion to the 470ft (142m) height. Nothing intrudes in the uninterrupted vista over the Highland Boundary Fault and into the high hills beyond. Between the Ochils in the east and the Clyde westward, the view encompasses the Perthshire Hills such as Ben More and Stobinian, round to the prominent Ben Lomond, Ben Vorlich (next left) and on to The Cobbler, and the Cowal Hills further west. But it is the loch and its islands that are most striking. Sea shells have been found in the terminal moraines, the materials dumped by glaciers, at the south end of the loch. This suggests that before the last Ice Age, the sea intruded up the Vale of Leven, seen conspicuously left. The last advance of the glaciers caused a wide dam of deposited material to form after they finally melted and withdrew. Only 27ft (8m) above sea level, Loch Lomond thus nearly became a sea loch like nearby Loch Long, a long fjord pointing far into the hills.

STONEYMOLLAN - LOCH LOMOND VIEWS
4 miles (6.5km)   Easy, but on moderate gradient; no dogs

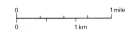

This is a walk missed by most visitors whizzing up the A82 Loch Lomond route. It shows how suddenly the countryside changes, from the industrial and housing estates of the Vale of Leven to the wilder moorlands of the Highland edge. Although it is a there-and-back-again route, keeping to the right of way, the views are splendid, and it would make a fine summer evening walk, should you be staying in the vicinity. This is sheep country, so, please **no dogs**.

1 *Finding the starting point is the trickiest part of the walk. It lies on the old main road. You must first get to the roundabout situated between the bridge over the River Leven and the A811's junction with the A82 (which is also a roundabout, at the end of the dual carriagway, if coming from Dumbarton.) If coming along the dual carriageway, go right at the junction roundabout and left at the next. If coming from the east along the A811, go right at the second of the Balloch roundabouts. At the time of writing, the old main road going north towards Loch Lomond is signed for the caravan park. Park by the roadside beyond the caravan park seen on your left. (N.B. From the Dumbarton direction, just before the junction roundabout, the footbridge you will be crossing at the start of the walk is seen ahead.)*

8 *Go through another gate at the end of the plantation. Walk a little way down the track, then on to the slope on your left for the last viewpoint.*

9 *Retrace your steps to your parking place.*

7 *Go through the gate and enter the conifer plantation.*

6 *Stay near the boundary fence, keeping it on your right.*

5 *At Upper Stoneymollan, you leave the tarred road behind, going straight ahead through a gate. The woodland is also left behind as the landscape changes to a pleasant, open, brackeny hillside with a burn flowing down on the left.*

4 *Cross the bridge and bear right uphill (not sharp right, a private driveway).*

3 *Go straight along this road till you reach the pedestrian footbridge over the main Loch Lomond road.*

2 *Look for the road on the left called 'Lower Stoneymollan Road' between two cottages. It is just after the caravan park.*

A The views of Loch Lomond improve the higher you walk up this tarred road.

B Sheep country. With the sheep's close nibbling of grasses, bracken thrives where they graze, its seed carried on their fleeces.

C Forestry. Another cash-crop takes priority. Pause to look back to the Highland Boundary Fault, running its knobbly way along the line of the islands and into Conic Hill, Walk 27. (All this is below, i.e., right of Ben Lomond, the most conspicuous mountain in view.) The change from Old Red Sandstone (southwards) to harder Dalradian Schists (northwards) can be traced by the hummocks that run to the horizon, north-eastwards. Note, further left, the distant hills of upper Balquhidder, still to the right of Ben Lomond.

D Looking ahead and westwards, the profile of the Arran Hills (the so-called 'Sleeping Warrior') lies on the horizon to the south-west beyond the River Clyde and Port Glasgow.

THE WHANGIE
3 miles (5km)   Moderate; no dogs

The Whangie has been well-known to generations of Glasgow rock-climbers. This strange geological phenomenon offers a wide variety of short but interesting pitches. For the walker it has scenic attractions, too, and is ideal for a short afternoon or evening's walk, enjoying views of Loch Lomond from these northern slopes of the Kilpatrick Hills. As for the geological reason for this peculiar, slightly eerie, even claustrophobic cleft, one explanation is an earthquake, while the information notice at the start of the walk also suggests glacial plucking. (This is stage one in the formation of a corrie, which is itself the hollow or valley scooped out of the side of a mountain by the passage of a glacier. Extremes of temperature at the head of the valley freeze rock slabs into the ice, which then 'plucks' them away and down the line of the glacier.) There is a third explanation for the geological peculiarities of The Whangie. The Devil was in such a state of anticipation as he flew to a witches' meeting somewhere in the north, that he lashed his tail and carved off the rock slice through which the path now goes. It might even explain the odd atmosphere that surrounds the place, though given a fine evening you might not notice it. Concentrate instead on the larks, the curlews and the Queen's View from the car park, where you will have to leave your dog. It is also the place, because of its popularity, to see fashion footwear at its worst. Do not attempt this walk in high heels.

A Note the hump of Dumgoyne, eastwards on the edge of the Fintry Hills.

B The view from the path, hemmed in between the fence below and the crags on your left, improves as you make your way towards The Whangie, as yet unseen. This is skylark country. Note the other little hump of Duncryne Hill, beyond the Stockie Muir, the moorland straight ahead, but in front of Loch Lomond to the north-west.

C Considering the nearness of the city of Glasgow, from the triangulation point there is a wide prospect over wild moorland, with Dumbarton Muir and the Kilpatricks to west and south.

D You are now inside The Whangie with vertical rock walls rising on both sides. There is a gap that gives a fine view north-west to Loch Lomond.

E The small birds that show grey, buff, a black eye-stripe and a conspicuous white rump are wheatears, common in summer along this section. The bird's name is derived from Anglo-Saxon and literally means 'white-arse'.

F For full details of the range of hills visible, check the excellent viewpoint indicator in the car-park.

Over

0   1 mile

0   1 km

8 As you re-emerge, take the lowest path that you can find, going right and back along the face of the hill, retracing your footsteps to the ladder stile and down to the car park.

1 The walk starts from a well-marked parking place and large car park about 7 miles (11.2km) north of Bearsden, Glasgow, on the A809 to Drymen. Alternatively, if travelling from Drymen, look for the site about 6 miles (9.6km) to the south, on the right.

7 You enter by an unpromising-looking path which seems to disappear into the rock face.

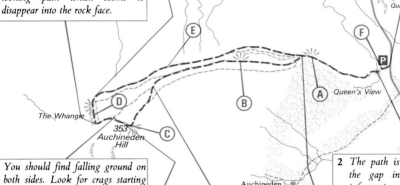

6 You should find falling ground on both sides. Look for crags starting again on your right. This is the 'back door' of The Whangie.

2 The path is unmistakable: though the gap in the wall, past the information notice and uphill to the conifers ahead on the skyline.

5 A number of trails wonder away from the triangulation point. If you go straight ahead, towards two reservoirs, then you will overshoot The Whangie and have to descend a steep west-facing section after only a few minutes, then divert sharp right along a faint path. It is better to leave the top by going half-right on a path that leads off in a westerly direction.

4 Check that you are on a path which rises above a second line of rocks which start below you, right. As you near the top, a path comes in to join from your left. This is the one mentioned in point 3 that runs along the hill-top. Continue to triangulation point on Auchineden Hill.

3 With most of the uphill section over, you reach a ladder stile; go over it. From here a number of paths diverge, including one that runs along the top of the line of crags that goes off to your left. In unkind weather, however, it is easier to take the path that runs along the foot of these rocks. Do not lose height.

OVERTOUN AND THE KILPATRICKS
3-9 miles (5-14 km), depending upon route   Easy (low loop) to Moderate

The policies of Overtoun Estate offer countryside pleasures only minutes from Dumbarton and the A82. Further uphill in Forestry Commission ground, the walk around the Lang Craigs opens up views extending from the Renfrew Hills and the Clyde Estuary to the panorama of Loch Lomond. **Note:** no dogs allowed at Overtoun, and stout footwear should be worn if continuing to the Lang Craigs, where younger children should be closely supervised by a responsible adult. There are several options for this walk, giving a choice between a short stroll or a longer ramble. Starting from the Police Headquarters off the A82, the easy loop around the Overtoun policies can be enjoyed on its own, or linked into a longer walk continuing to the Lang Craigs viewpoint. Alternatively, the Craigs can be approached more directly from Milton, just outside Dumbarton on the A82.

3 There is a choice of either driveway or footpath beside Overtoun Burn. If on the driveway, you eventually leave it by turning right through a picnic area, when close to a large farmhouse on the left.

4 Path climbs steeply up steps, left to Spardie Linn, a waterfall.

5 Cross footbridge on right, noting the sandstone in the stream bed above the falls, and follow the path upstream to regain the driveway. Cross the burn by the impressive bridge leading to Overtoun House. N.B. cars can be taken as far as Overtoun House by turning north off the A82 at Milton, opposite the garage. Now continue along the driveway as it bears right around the house to reach the estate entrance at a sharp bend in the minor road up from Milton.

2 Walking to the A82, go right, past the Police Headquarters, then immediately right again, through the old gates of Overtoun Estate. Continue up the pedestrian-only path, crossing over a housing estate road and entering the policies proper.

6 From here, you can easily return to your starting point by turning right, see point 14 overleaf. Otherwise, carry on up the road ahead, passing Loch Bowie on your right. Beyond the loch, at a sharp Y-junction, turn left and go uphill. (N.B. this section of the walk can also be approached by parking at Milton and walking up Milton Brae, opposite the garage on the A82, following part of the road to the car park at Overtoun House mentioned above.)

1 Park on the north side of the A82 dual carriageway west of Dumbuck Quarry, between the Pinetrees Hotel and the Police Headquarters in an estate of wood-faced houses. Take care on the busy main road.

Over

12 *Path and fence lead up beyond the forest and on to the rim of the Lang Craigs where there are red grouse and spectacular views. Keeping the fence between you and the cliff face, continue by the path along the tops, crossing an intervening forestry fence by a stile. WARNING: This is no place for very small children.*

11 *Noting a small waterfall in the gorge on your right, follow the path for about ¼ mile (½ km) to a wire fence with a stile. DO NOT CONTINUE ACROSS THE STILE, but turn left, following the smaller path, which becomes clearer further on uphill with the fence on your right.*

10 *After a mile or so of gentle climbing, the track ends at Black Linn Reservoir, on your right, with the cone of Doughnot Hill appearing beyond the trees. Take the smaller path in front of you, with the fence on your right for 20 -30 yards (18 -27 m), before the path veers left through a break in the trees. (Doughnot Hill should now be on your right.) N.B. from this point on, the path can be slippery and boggy in damp weather.*

13 *The Craigs turn south. Path swings left, below a rocky bluff. Cross a second fence by a stile. Path cuts left and uphill, then right and picks up fenceline again (60 yards/55m). Continue down by the fence and then a wall bearing right to regain first gate crossed at start of upper loop. Retrace steps to Y-junction. Go left down road to Milton, or right to entrance to Overtoun House.*

14 *If returning to the A82 near the Police Headquarters, turn downhill from the Overtoun gateway and then follow the track till it narrows and becomes a path. Keep heading downhill to the estate adjoining the main road. Turn right, past the Pinetrees Hotel, and it is a couple of minutes to your starting point.*

9 *Continue following the main track through the coniferous plantations, passing reservoirs first on your right and then to the left.*

8 *With quarry on right, and fence left, continue uphill past a brick hut. Track crosses an iron gate, then fords the burn by stepping stones, before striking uphill across a second gate towards forestry plantations. The Craigs are now visible ahead to your left.*

7 *Follow the road uphill to Greenland Farm. Then bear left by the metalled track which continues uphill to reach quarry workings. Take a rest here and look back; you should begin to see Renfrewshire, the Clyde Estuary and even Loch Lomond.*

Map labels: Round Wood, Overtoun Burn, Quarry, Sheepfold, Lang Craigs, Waterfall, Black Linn Reservoir, Reservoir, Aqueduct, Overtoun House, Reservoir, Spardie Linn, Police Headquarters, Reservoir, Quarry, Loch Bowie, Quarry, Greenland Farm, Dumbarton, Dumbarton Castle, A814, Milton, A82

A By the burnside, note the ruins of a power-house, remains of an early example of hydro-electric power for domestic use.

B The rock at Spardie Linn is known as Spout of Ballagan sandstone (from a prominent outcrop in the

Campsies). This forms a lip over which the water tumbles, wearing away the soft shales and cementstones beneath.

C The views from the Lang Craigs are remarkable for a relatively small hill. Dumbarton Rock and the Vale

of Leven communities are clear below, with Glasgow spreading out to the south-east and Greenock and Gourock across the Clyde Estuary. Best of all is the open view right up Loch Lomond, as it runs north into the Highlands.

Walk 34

THE LOCH SLOY DAM
7 miles (11.5km)   Easy; no dogs

Escape from the hubbub of the Loch Lomond traffic into the slightly unexpected tranquillity of a glen with looming mountains. Admittedly the scenery is marred by power lines in plenty - but the scale of the rocks and hills is large enough to dwarf even a 182 feet (56m) high dam, built in 1946, the first major project of the North of Scotland Hydro-Electric Board. The dam generates 130MW of electricity and meant the raising of Loch Sloy by 155 feet (47m), drowning for ever the old home-lands of the Clan MacFarlane in order to supply power to Central Scotland. In spite of these changes, the walk has much to recommend it and gives an opportunity to sample the wildness of the interior from the 'security' of a good road. You will not have to pay too much attention to navigation - there are more views than instructions - and the route is on a surfaced road nearly all the way, which you will only have to share with the occasional NSHEB service vehicle and more ambitious walkers heading for the tops of the looming 'Munros'. Like Walk 21, Glen Gyle, you could even take a push-chair! **Dogs are not advised - this is sheep country.**

A The Inveruglas Power Station with its less-than-beautiful four steel pipes (pre-dating the days of scenic consciousness!) receives water from Loch Sloy via a tunnel on the hill 2 miles (3.22km) long. The water drives four vertical turbo-alternators and then escapes into Loch Lomond.

B After noting the big hills that begin to dominate the landscape, you reach a strange humming complex behind wire on your left. This is a switching station. Power arrives here not only from Inveruglas but from two other hydro-electric schemes further west (in Glen Shira and upper Glen Fyne). It leaves via yet more pylons that stride south down Glen Loin, on your left, beyond the station.

C The nearest mountains are, left and continuously visible as you climb, A' Chrois (the end of a ridge that runs from Beinn Narnain); Ben Vane, conspicuous ahead, beyond the farm; the top of Ben Vorlich hiding behind the rocky shoulder immediately on your right; Beinn Ime, set further back in the glen between A' Chrois and Ben Vane.

D The dam is 1,170 feet (357m) long and 295,000 tonnes of crushed rock were used in the concrete. It was the first buttress-type dam in Scotland. Among those employed in its construction were prisoners of war awaiting repatriation, following the end of World War II. A temporary railway station was set up at Inveruglas to receive them.

E You then have a view of the dammed loch itself. Its shoreline scar is an inevitable result of the fluctuations in the water level. The catchment area was increased from 6.5 square miles (17sq km) to 31 square miles (80sq km) by means of tunnels and aqueducts. This is, admittedly, one of the wettest parts of Scotland - if it rains, remember that every inch of rain generates one million units of electricity!

F The insect-eating sundew is quite common in places among the mosses in the shallow ditch along the upper side of the road. Among the bird life, wheatears, with their distinctive white rumps, are also very conspicuous.

G On your way down there are fine views of the impressive cone of Ben Lomond. Equally impressive is the fact that during the last Ice Age, which ended a mere 10,000 years ago, a glacier carved out the trough of Loch Lomond right across the former watershed of the Inveruglas Water. This burn, which is the main one on your right as you make your way down the glen, would once have emptied itself eastwards, beyond Inversnaid, into Loch Katrine.

H Lower down, Inversnaid itself can be seen across the loch.

I Finally, as you reach the car park at the end of your walk, look out, right, to Inveruglas Isle, with the remains of a MacFarlane castle, sacked by Cromwell.

Over

6 *If you wish to see to the other side of it, follow the road round and uphill, past the buildings. Just before you reach the tunnel, detour left, leaving the path and going up and right, round the hillock through which the tunnel is driven.* **DO NOT go into the tunnel**.

7 *Retrace your steps to the road, which now, followed in the reverse direction, gives a completely different set of views. Consider how the Clan MacFarlane lived here, hemmed in by intimidating mountains, but with a comparatively rich pasture land, bright and green, on which to graze their cattle. Their war-cry was 'Loch Sloy', though it has changed much since their departure two hundred years ago.*

1 *Start from the large viewpoint car park on the shores of Loch Lomond, on the A82 just north of the Inveruglas Power Station, on the right. Turn left out of the car park and make your way back down the road, past the power station. Take care on the busy road, but there is a pavement or verge nearly all the way.*

5 *Walk up to the dam, where the road turns left across its base.*

4 *After the farm called Coiregrogain, (which can be seen off to the left of the road) go straight on at the road junction to see the dam. It comes into view ahead as the road swings north with the bulk of Ben Vane looming on your left. You also lose sight of Beinn Ime, behind Vane's shoulder.*

3 *Go straight on, past the switching station, at the junction of three roads, i.e., take the middle road.*

2 *After Inveruglas Farm, on the left, turn right into a driveway, conspicuous by its notices warning about no parking, no unauthorised vehicles, no dogs on the hill. Go through the gate and under the railway bridge. This is on the main road to the dam. Continue up.*

Map labels: Loch Sloy · Beinn Dubh 773 · Dam · Weir · E · D · Tunnel · Inveruglas Water · Ben Vane 915 · F · C · Generating Station · A · Power Station · Inveruglas · Inveruglas Isle · P · Coiregrogain · Switching Station · Inveruglas Farm · I · Inversnaid Hotel · G · B · H · A' Chrois · Loch Lomond · A82

INVERARNAN - LOCH LOMOND VIEWS

4.5 miles (7.5km)   Moderate (easy in places); no dogs

```
0                    1 mile
0         1 km
```

A walk that takes advantage of an attractive part of the West Highland Way to gain a wonderful end-on view of Loch Lomond. It lies near ancient ways through the hills, used by cattle-drovers before the coming of the railways ended their trade.

The area once supplied timber for iron smelting; the old Caledonian pine forest reached one of its most southerly limits in nearby glen Falloch. Later, after the tourists arrived, the river that runs parallel to the walk described here was canalised between the end of Loch Lomond and the Inverarnan Hotel. Steamers connected with stagecoaches at the hotel, which is also your starting point.

2   *Taking care on the main road, turn right from the car park and walk a few hundred yards along the road as far as the first bridge over the River Falloch. Turn right, cross the bridge and go right again over a stile. At time of writing this had West Highland Way indicators.*

1   *The Inverarnan Hotel has welcomed generations of walkers and climbers and is on the right as you go north, on the A82 beyond where Loch Lomond ends and Glen Falloch begins. Park in the car park.*

3   *Continue along the pleasant river bank till the path meets the Ben Glas Burn (which has a fine waterfall much higher up the hillside). Then turn upstream and over a tall ladder-stile.*

4   *Turn right over stile and cross the newish footbridge, built by the Royal Engineers. Follow the path south till it almost rejoins the River Falloch.*

5   *Path forks; go upwards and left.*

6   *Go through the ruined walls of the hamlet of Blarstainge, evidence that this deserted east side of Glen Falloch once supported a much higher population.*

7   *As you approch the Dubh Lochan, the 'little black loch' on your right, look out for a diversion, newly made at time of writing and intended to prevent path damage. The sign takes you upwards to the left, off the original path which stayed on the level.*

8   *You may wish to make this a longer expedition by continuing down, eventually to reach the oak woods by the loch itself. There are also views across to Ardlui. Otherwise, retrace your steps back to Inverarnan.*

A If walking this route (and most other walks in this book) in moist weather in springtime, there may be a pleasing scent in the greenest of woodland, which does not come from any blossom. This is the scent given off by new birch leaves. You may notice it now as the path climbs into the birches.

B High above and out of sight, left, is the old drovers' route down to Glen Gyle from Glen Falloch. Rob Roy would have known it well.

C In the wetter patches, butterwort, an insectivorous plant (like sundew) may be found. It looks like a little fleshy green starfish.

D From the hamlet, looking northwards up Glen Falloch, Ben Lui and Ben Oss are conspicuous, as is the nearer Ben Vorlich, southwards and on the other side of Loch Lomond.

E From the top, a magnificent view of Loch Lomond, lying in its narrow glacial trough, open out. Island I Vow is conspicuous.